Divine Economy Model

How to Make Your Thoughts and Actions Powerful and Harmonious

Bruce Koerber

Cover design by Matthew Holdridge

Typesetting and ebook design by Mike Dworski

ISBN: 978-0-9960955-3-2 (Print)
ISBN: 978-0-9960955-4-9 (ebook)

This book is dedicated to the lives lost from the beginning of time because of ignorance or hatred.

Contents

Foreword

How are we, as individuals, to think about economics and about the economy? The economy is made to seem like something so big—the sum total of all people's economic actions and interactions and transactions—and so complex as to be daunting. And economics—the science by which we try to understand the economy—is for PhD's and advanced mathematicians.

Well, first, we *should* all think about the economy. It is an important element of the environment in which we live and work. It's a system in which we all have an active role. It provides each of us with opportunities both to help ourselves and to help others. Those two opportunities combine together in economics.

And the truth is that we all have the capability to understand and make sense of the economy through the use of mental models.

Mental models are available to all of us. They enable us to simplify and organize the complex information we get from the world around us. They are an important—in fact, critical—contributor to how we live our lives, and how we make sense of the world. In the search for purpose and meaning amidst unfathomable complexity, mental models can guide us. Without them, information might overwhelm us.

How do we construct a useful mental model? The key is to identify what's essential for understanding, and discard those levels of detail that add more to complexity than they do to clarity.

In other words, to be useful, models must be concise (not too many variables), simply constructed (so that everyone who interacts with them can understand their workings), and clearly applicable in the full-scale world. When designed this way, models serve the very high purposes of facilitating deep understanding and more informed interaction with the system.

From Theory to Application

In what way are models applicable to the real world? The science of Austrian economics provides us the medium for translating theory into practice: purposeful human behavior.

We all exhibit purposeful behavior: we choose the ends we prefer to aim at, and we choose the means we judge to be best suited to achieve those ends. The ends are always about making things better. We seek to become better people, through achievement, discovery, adventure, hard work, empathy for others, collaboration, invention, entrepreneurship, trustworthiness, or some other combination of values. We learn lessons from the successes and failures of others, and we try to put that learning into practice through improved decision-making, shrewder choices, and more emphasis on what appears to work versus what doesn't.

We also learn that we can all do better when we collaborate than when we fight with each other. Even economic competition is a collaboration, a discovery process, as F. A. Hayek famously called it, in which people rival each other to find the best way to collaborate and to prove their way to others.

Institutions and Values

Human collaboration leads to the emergence of institutions, norms of behavior that bind us softly together in the practices that bring economic prosperity. We can all experience material rewards and pleasures, we can feel better about our relationships with others, we can identify a role for ourselves, and we can carve out our own purpose and meaning, and we can achieve all those individual benefits through collaboration.

Values such as ambition, driving individuals to achievement, are balanced with responsibility and self-control, for cohesion of the group. Imagination and courage drive the discovery and innovation underpinning economic growth and prosperity, while love and mutual respect keep the discoverers and innovators connected to those who are the maintainers of the status quo. A balanced portfolio of values helps us to be dynamic and cohesive at the same time.

Complexity Made Understandable

The genius of the book you are about to read is to make the most complex adaptive system mankind has created, the economy, understandable through the medium of an original mental model. You'll find a code to follow, a breakdown of the most important elements, then a re-assembly of those elements into a complete system, and an inspiration for your own vision and your own participation. You'll find the ethics of the market and the purposeful action of entrepreneurship for all. You'll understand how there can be continuous advance both for you and all other participants in the economy.

Bruce Koerber is an author who is deeply committed to helping all of us make sense of economics and the economy. He performs the invaluable service of elucidation and clarification. He provides a framework in which we can understand our own roles, the roles of others and the impact of action, of processes and of time. We can see how we fit in, as he puts it in Chapter 4.

Economics is humanist, a science of people. The Divine Economy provides a new perspective on that humanism.

Hunter Hastings
hunterhastings.com

Introduction

A PICTURE IS WORTH A THOUSAND WORDS

Writing this book was ... a step forward.

Imagine yourself being able to visualize the economy at any moment and being able to see how the economy absorbs the characteristics of the surrounding circumstances and being able to understand the natural flow of the processes taking place. To most of us that would be what it feels like to be a wise person. That aspiration is not out of reach since the model you will soon read about is one that is conceptual and visual and logical.

It is not your fault if you find it hard to see the value of economics—because everything seems so disjointed. Even though you are fully aware that all things are interconnected you are expected to make sense of the fragmented pieces of information that seem foreign and contradictory to one another. It is no wonder why you, like most of us, end up losing interest in economics with a distant hope that someone else will find out how it's all supposed to work.

Turning the economy over to someone else is a scary thought, don't you think? Whether you understand it or not the economy is vital and impacts us like nothing else. It turns out the economy is not something incomprehensible or impersonal. Instead it is your friend and it is fascinating and it is as easy to understand as a few visualizations.

Empowering you is not what those who are trying to control the economy want. One way to keep you weak is to perpetuate the false belief that the economy belongs in the realm of 'experts'. Don't forget: that is precisely a thought that ran through your mind and that is what made you shy away from grasping the economy by the forelock with confidence!

It is confidence and certitude and vision that annihilates the barriers that have been put in our way. Now not only will you be a force to be reckoned with but the frail and hollow and poisonous shell of 'economics' that is being pushed as 'scientific' will crumble under its own weight of falsity. Instead of being victims of control and manipulation we will be the agents of creativity and productivity and purposefulness. No more top down oppression. You will have the insight it takes to move the world forward.

The divine economy theory that is contained in four core books has now been out there in the market for quite a while but often people don't want to spend time learning theory. They just want the nugget of gold! Giving you the gold nugget is what this book does. It pulls from each one of the four books the model at its center, which all of the surrounding theory describes and supports.

The First Spark

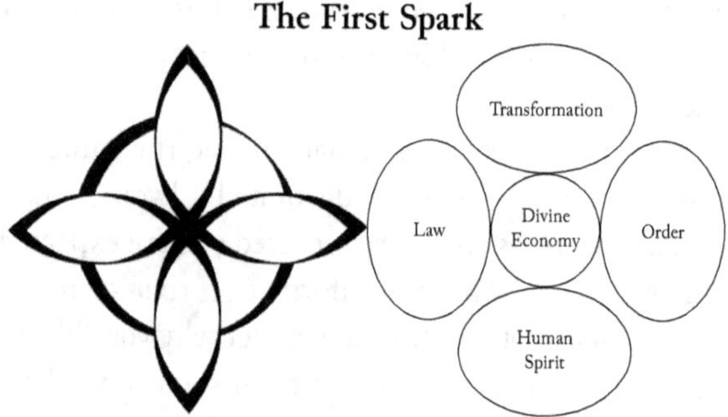

That is what is so important about this book because people want to know how economics applies to them? and how they can put it into action? Since we all see things from our own point of view the answers to those questions are unique for every person which again proves the importance of this book since the models are visual and conceptual. It is like the thrill and magnificence of fine art. It appeals uniquely to each person and inspires them to their own greatness.

There are four chapters in this book. In the first chapter you will be introduced to and experience the macroeconomic model which appears in "More Than Laissez-Faire". By the end of Chapter 1 you will be able to visualize how the economy works.

The second chapter in this book will show you the microeconomic model that is at the heart of "The Human Essence of Economics" book. By the end of Chapter 2 you will know where value comes from and how to create value.

The third chapter takes you on a journey into the world of ethical economics by exploring the model that is described in "Ethical Economics for Today and Tomorrow". At the end of Chapter 3 you will see where the economy came from and where it is going.

The final chapter is extracted from "Liberty & Justice of Economic Equilibrium" and from Chapter 4 you will learn how to be an assayer of justice and appreciate the power and providence of economic equilibrium.

Now dive in and return often to refresh yourself. This ocean is vast and powerful and rhythmic. It will always be there for you to revisit.

Chapter 1

Imagining the Economy as a Whole*

Imagine an organic economy that is capable of serving every human being on the planet. With the blink of an eye you see yourself intimately and wholly integrated and actively helping to shape the future for yourself and others. The transformation you seek makes you a better person in so many ways and that is what you see happening for everyone else too.

It wasn't too long ago (and maybe still) that you felt apathetic about the world situation. You may have come to the conclusion that most of your efforts went up in smoke as a result of the lack of human cohesiveness. All of this diffusion of will, that results from a lack of vision, certainly makes any of your feelings of success seem elusive and hollow.

The world is not going to end! The economy is not something that can ever be destroyed. It has an inherent power that is underappreciated and underestimated.

That doesn't mean that there aren't those out there who are doing harm to the economy, nor does it mean there aren't those who have the perverse intention of trying to destroy the economy. In fact, it often feels like they are winning.

As you will soon find out the enemies of the economy are up against a formidable foe, one that is incomprehensibly powerful. And you happen to be a part of the vanguard.

Now you will see the flash of a spark that when it comes into contact with kindling, the kindling of minds that are searching to understand economics, will catch fire and turn into a blaze:

---

*This is an excerpt from Chapter 2 of my book "More Than Laissez-Faire".

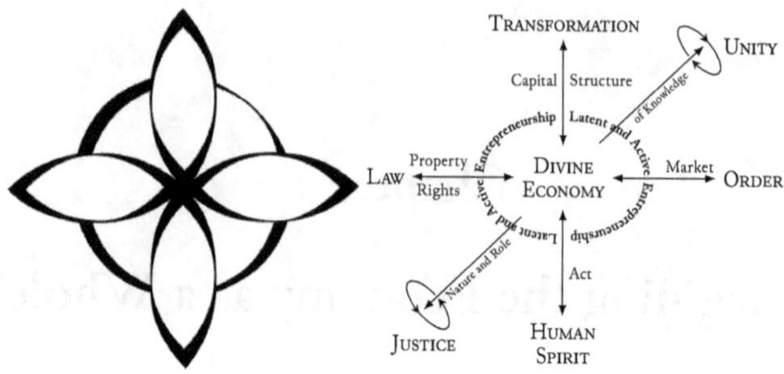

This chapter shows you the macroeconomic model. By the end of this chapter you will be able to visualize in your mind's eye how the economy works.

Divine Economy Model ©

Organic and subjective and splendid!

The Code

Shortly I will begin to present to you a graphical representation of the divine economy model. But before we begin examining the model we will want to understand the conceptual basis of what is called the Cartesian coordinate system. In mathematics the applications of the two-dimensional coordinate system and of the three-dimensional coordinate system appear to be very empirical. Despite being used mostly for empirical work the Cartesian coordinate system is not restricted from more conceptual applications, as proven when it is expanded to higher dimensions, for example, the fourth dimension, the fifth dimension or even to the *n*th 'degrees of freedom.'

I take advantage of the conceptual potentialities of the Cartesian coordinate system and use it as a part of the design of my subjective model. Just as the higher dimensions are abstract I make all of the dimensions of my model abstract. Referring to the Cartesian coordinate system, Bernhard Riemann in 1854 described the value of this abstraction: "Abstract studies such as these allow one to observe relationships without being limited by narrow terms, and prevent traditional prejudices from inhibiting one's progress." In my model the two-dimensional system is subjective or 'abstract' as is the third dimension and the fourth dimension and the fifth dimension, in other words, my model is five-dimensional.

The Conceptual Model

Now I will introduce the divine economy model to you. As the model is presented; its interconnectedness, reciprocity and symmetry will be discussed. One analogy that may prove useful is that of a complex organism made up of components that are more or less differentiated. Ourselves, we are made up of systems and organs and tissues and cells. Likewise the divine economy model has universal laws, foundational elements, concepts, and principles.

The center of the model is its reality and essence, summed up using the words 'divine economy.' These two powerful words clearly state the vital perspective of this model. These two words efficiently convey the source and the dominion. The implication here is far more magnificent than laissez-faire which merely suggests 'not to meddle.' The implication here is that the economy is above and beyond our human understanding and that it can be and is corrupted by human intervention alone.

The divine economy is both pervasive and subtle and its dominion reaches everyone in their daily affairs. It is basic and connected to the necessary acts of every man and woman and by its conveyance of information it allows people to function.

The Two-Dimensional Model

Just as there are four cardinal directions; a north and south and east and west, the organic divine economy model has four petals. Gleaned from the knowledge and insight of many great thinkers I chose the following petals for the model: human spirit, transformation, law, and order. What we have is the model in its simplest form (see Diagram 2a).

To the model we then add reciprocity and symmetry (Diagram 2b). From now on you will notice arrows on both ends of the lines to represent reciprocity and symmetry. The element of reciprocity adds the

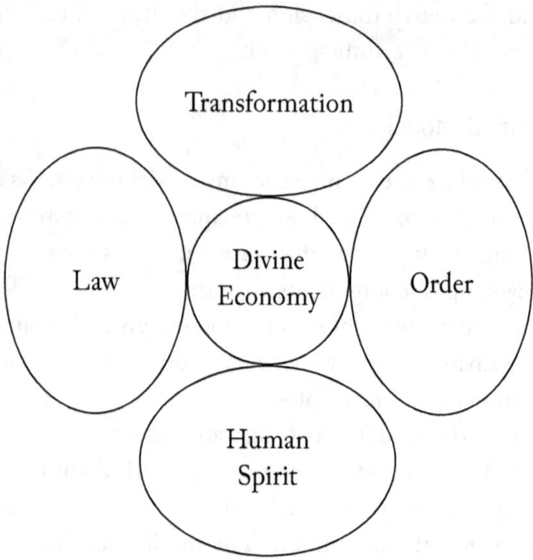

Diagram 2a: Anatomy of the divine economy

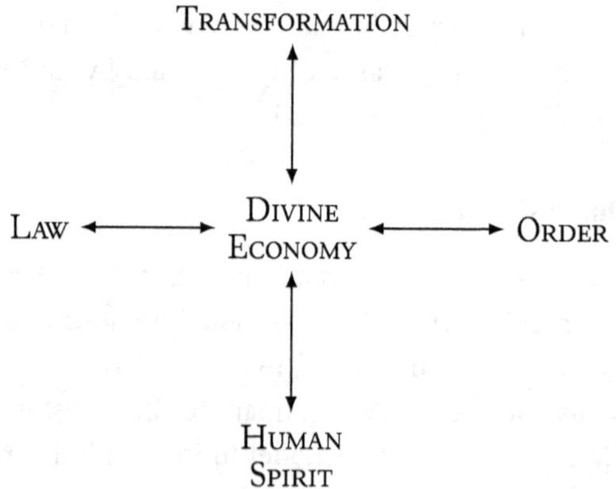

Diagram 2b: Skeletal structure of the divine economy

dimension of mutual exchange. Another way to describe what happens during an exchange is to see exchange as the fulfillment of the double inequality of wants. I want what you have more than what I have and you reciprocate those feelings, therefore we exchange.

Proportionality and relativity manifest themselves in the world via the element of symmetry. For example, as transformation within the economy increases the other vital elements of the economy also increase and the economy as a whole increases. The model now becomes what is seen in Diagram 2b.

In this form the functionality of the model begins to emerge. It has a dynamic nature. Every point is relative to every other point and every understanding gained causes movement, advancing civilization.

To continue to improve the functionality of the model more scientific elements of the economy are added. These economic elements were discovered by great thinkers in the tradition of classical liberalism. These certain points of focus are added to the skeletal structure as intermediary potencies.

To the skeleton we add more substance making the model more realistic and bringing it to life. To the human spirit appendage we add action, purposeful action. To the transformation appendage we add capital structure. The law appendage fills out nicely with property rights and it is the market that beefs up the order appendage.

With this added substance, as shown in Diagram 2c, it begins to become evident to us how the model neatly incorporates the intermediary elements that make it operational. Using the analogies of a skeletal structure and appendages reminds us about the organic nature of the model.

This is the highest form of the two-dimensional model and this is where the model begins to become complex. We will have to take a step back and examine more deeply the foundational components. Then the extremely potent intermediary elements will need to be explored.

Going back to the skeletal structure of the divine economy in Diagram 2b it is easy to see how interactive and cumulatively interactive it is. The human being has a nature that is subject to illumination. It is the human spirit that reflects that reality. Transformation is the illu-

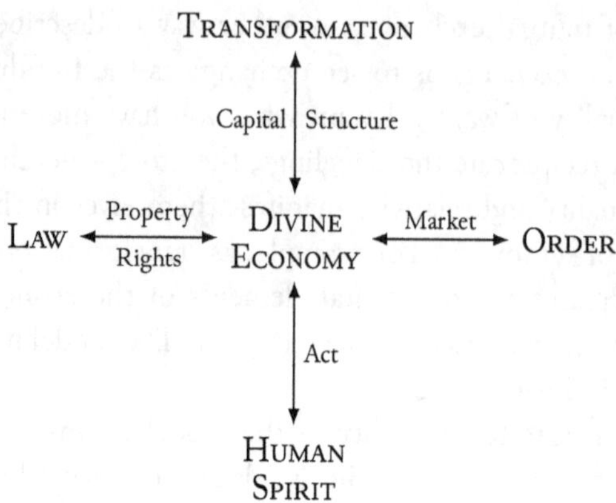

Diagram 2c: Modus operandi of the divine economy

mination that takes place. This all comes about because we encounter the human spirit of others, directly or indirectly. The world is not a vacuum, people learn from others and from their environment.

The world has structure and incorporating structure into our lives creates order. Transformation is furthered by discovering the operational laws of that order. Completing the circle, then, the human spirit is illumined by the transformation that has taken place.

The dynamic interaction of all of these interrelated elements is certain. Already it is clear that the complexity of the divine economy is mind boggling. We have to trust in its divine nature and content ourselves with understanding bits and pieces, ever humbled by the infinite greatness of the divine economy.

Now moving on to the more complex model in Diagram 2c—the modus operandi of the divine economy—we need to spend some time educating and re-educating ourselves about these intermediary elements. It would be inaccurate and naïve to pretend that there is a common understanding of these four elements in the economic literature or in the minds of most readers.

The four scientific elements that make up the modus operandi of the divine economy are property rights, human action, the market, and capital structure. These are potent forces which universally permeate human life on this planet!

Placement of these intermediate elements into the model relative to the initial foundational components expands the foundation of the model. The model readily accommodates the fluid manner in which these eight elements all juxtapose themselves.

Property rights interface closely with human action, the market and the capital structure. Property rights are truly foundational and have a strong connection to law in the divine economy since they anchor the economy to the human being. In its most basic and primary expression, property rights are human rights. The existence of a human being grants dominion, and its peaceful expansion toward food, clothing and higher attainments all fall within the domain of property rights.

The human spirit—each one of us as a unique expression of the grace of God—becomes foundational in the divine economy through human action. Human action is the expression of the human spirit, which implies that the human spirit is the locus of communication and serves as a channel for the two-way flow of knowledge.

Understanding that the economy is a uniquely human institution means there is also cognition that the human spirit is where it all begins and human action is where it becomes manifest. Without human beings, whose nature it is to act purposefully, there would be no economy.

There is a saying: 'It takes two to tango!' That is what the market is. It is the place where the solitary individual becomes a social being.

By this very broad definition the interaction of parents with their children could even be considered a market. Although an argument could be forwarded against this line of reasoning but such an argument does not allow this very important point to be made therefore it serves no purpose here. The purpose of this broad definition is to remove the limiting definitions ascribed to the market and to remove the prejudices about the market.

The market is where individual human action undergoes reconfiguration into a more social entity. This is part of the dynamics between the 'act' and the 'transformation.' The market is where knowledge flows to and from in a civilization. And it is from this proverbial fountain of knowledge that order emerges. See Diagram 2d.

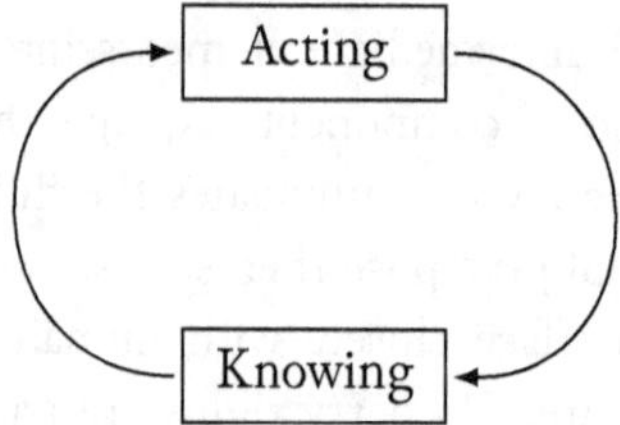

Diagram 2d: Proverbial fountain: part of the transformation process

The three scientific elements just described—property rights, human action, and the market—are inherent and found in full potential in the divine economy. The fourth element differs slightly from the others because of its very strong ties to time.

The fourth element, capital structure, is also foundational. It contains and conveys the knowledge that all things in this world are subject to the law of time. Capital is the means of stretching production beyond the present. It is necessary and foundational.

Most significantly, of all factors in the economy capital is the most limiting. See if you understand why. Ponder: in the here and now—in the present—we cannot live in the future! That is our limitation. The reason capital is the most limiting is because it is what connects the present and the future in the economy within 'our limitation.' It is constrained by uncertainty yet its variation or structure determines the transformation that takes place in the economy.

Since capital is the most limiting factor, the movement or advancement of civilization depends heavily upon the structure of capital. This necessitates, optimally, that the capital structure needs to be a harmonious expression of the market so it truthfully reflects the will of the people. In the divine economy fully vested human beings find and share knowledge in the market. Part of that knowledge reflects the importance of time which becomes manifest in capital and its relevant structure.

The Three-Dimensional Model

The next modification of the divine economy model stretches the imagination a little by adding a depth dimension, the third dimen-

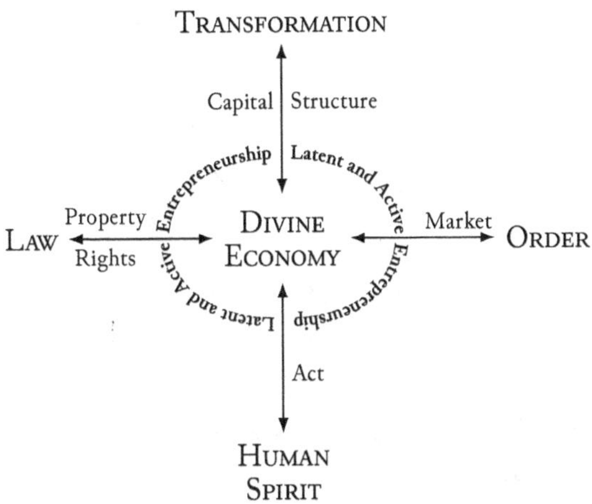

Diagram 2e: The driving force of the divine economy

sion in this model. This can be grasped fairly easily by imagining the modus operandi of the divine economy given in Diagram 2c as submerged in a bowl of water. The water that surrounds and supports the model represents latent and active entrepreneurship. See Diagram 2e.

Entrepreneurship is alertness to one's surroundings and the knowledge therein. This is nearly perfectly represented by the 'submersion' analogy. The water is what surrounds ('one's surroundings') and submersion into the water introduces entrepreneurship. In this entrepreneurial condition all that is within ('the knowledge therein') potentially comes to light.

When entrepreneurship is in the latent state the divine economy and its components are in potential only. When alertness triggers a response the result is active entrepreneurship, which significantly, is the driving force in the economy.

If I am in a latent state of entrepreneurship I may simply buy a product that I like. Or I may begin to actively perceive opportunities and compare & contrast to see what other products are out there to buy or sell. Additionally I may look at the time horizon. I may weigh the various possibilities and decide to save so that I can buy a tractor because of the prospect of improved production, for example.

As an active entrepreneur I may discover discrepancies in the market

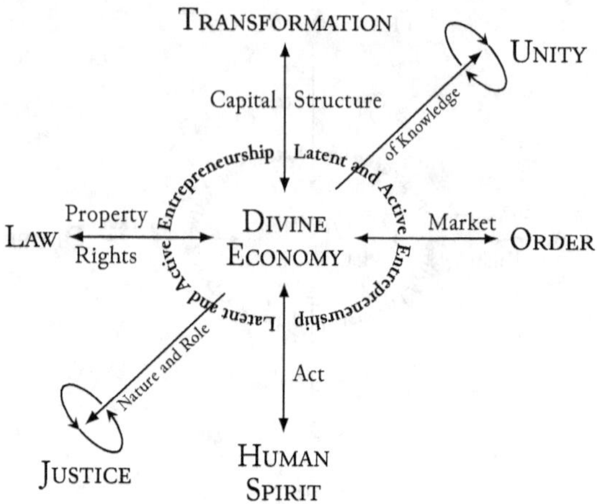

Diagram 2f: The complete Divine Economy Model independent of time

that lead to inefficiencies and I may take steps to remedy the situation. When in a latent state, the water merely holds within it the divine economy. But when there is active entrepreneurship, energy is released which charges all of the elements in the water.

The Fourth Dimension

The fourth dimension of the divine economy model enters into the picture by identifying its poles. The divine economy has many components just like Earth's complex system which has numerous components such as the water cycle, ocean currents, and geothermal forces to name a few. The Earth also can be understood more fully by examining these factors as they are influenced by rotation around its poles.

Similarly the divine economy can be more fully understood when the model includes the poles of unity and justice (Diagram 2f). It is around these two poles that the divine economy revolves. The axis of these poles represents the 'nature and role of knowledge.' The implication here—with this axis being centrally located within the model—is that knowledge flows throughout and that it is this free-flowing knowledge that best serves all of the divine economy processes.

This is a key concept in the divine economy theory. It is the nature and role of knowledge that enables the equilibrium forces to maintain balance and harmony. Intervention by those with finite human understanding strikes at the 'nature and role of knowledge' axis—with the consequences being a condition of imbalance and disharmony and a corruption of the divine economy.

To clarify the importance of justice, it is justice that inextricably links the interests of the individual and those of society. Justice also implies non-violence and non-coercion.

Elaborating on the pole of unity; the pole of unity shines with prosperity for all. There is now an awareness of the historical and scientific knowledge that shows all of humanity as one people. As far back as A.D. 1573 Bartolome de Albornoz wrote:

> Buying and selling is the nerve of human life that sustains the universe. By means of buying and selling the world is united, joining distant lands and nations, people of different languages, laws and ways of life.

The Fifth Dimension

The fifth dimension of the divine economy model brings in the reality of time since there is no realism to any economic model that is static. The dynamicism of all of the elements of the model comes to life as changes take place over time (Diagram 2g).

Statement: Now you can visualize (Diagram 2g) how the economy works.

See What Happens When You Take These Action Steps:

- Be a friend of the entrepreneurs and become an entrepreneur.
- Appreciate and use capital. Put it into action by way of savings and investment.
- Do what you can to safeguard property rights.
- Celebrate the transformative power of the economy.

Want to see how this extends into microeconomics? See Chapter 2.

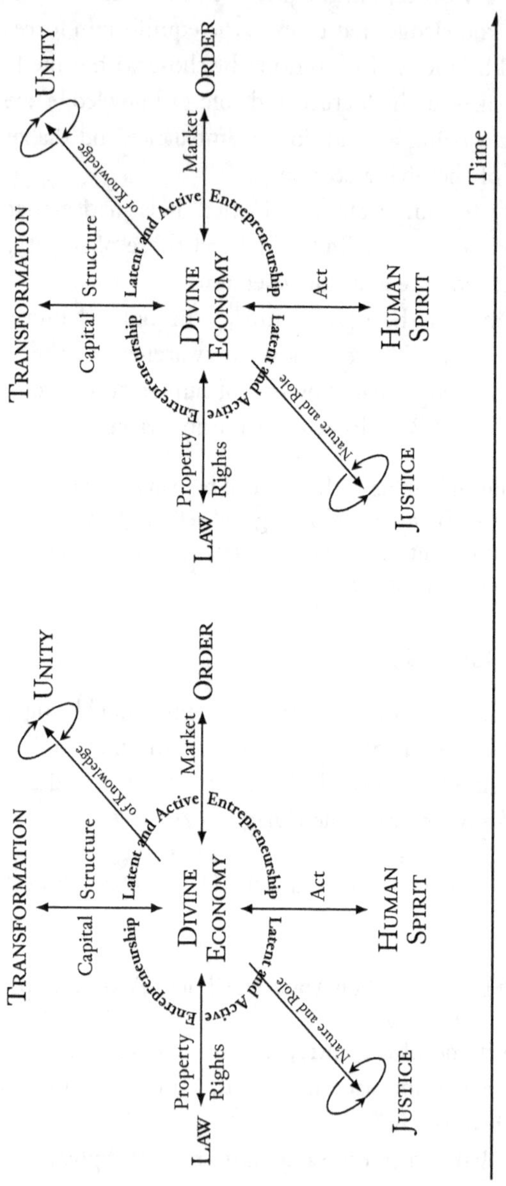

Diagram 2g: The complete Divine Economy Model over time

Chapter 2

Watching Your Dreams Come True*

You have, within you, creative powers most of which remain untapped. It's a matter of taking action on your dreams and working along with others to bring them to fruition. Your ability to create and produce are latent, at rest, just waiting for you to follow your dreams.

There is no certainty out there in the market, which means that trial and error is a natural process. There are no failures, only learning opportunities to gain wisdom along the road of pursuing your dreams. When you think about the adage "practice makes perfect" it is fairly easy to forget that early on in the process there were plenty of imperfections and failures. That is part of life and in many ways the spice of life.

Nothing is scary about finding out more about ourselves and at the same time finding out about others. That is what the market is all about and that leads to a better understanding about how it works. The nice thing about the market is that it is a universal reflection of human choices which shows that we are not so different after all.

Those without this healthy perspective don't want others to have the freedom to find their niche. Their lack of understanding of how the economy works makes them suspicious and obstructive. Their obstruction is simply one more obstacle to overcome but you have the creative ability to do exactly that.

While the obstructors distract themselves trying to extract meaning out of numbers you will be watching and listening to the valuation processes found in the dynamic market. You know where value comes from and you know what to do to add value all the while the obstruc-

*This is an excerpt from Chapter 2 of my book "The Human Essence of Economics".

tors have their heads down in the numbers, crunching them to no avail.

Now you will see the flash of a different spark that when it comes into contact with kindling, the kindling of minds that are searching for the source of value, will catch fire and turn into a blaze:

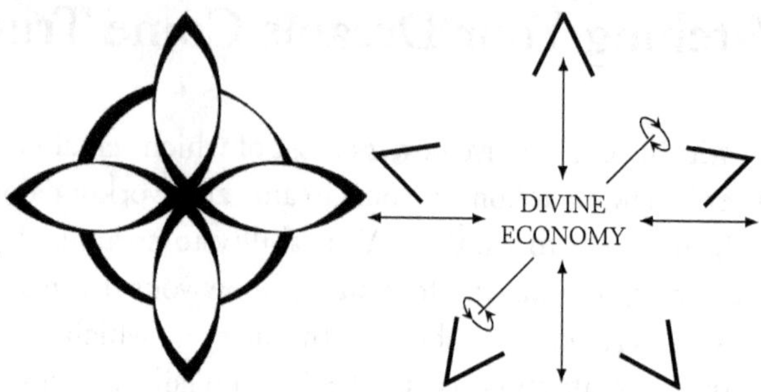

This chapter shows you the microeconomic model. By the end of this chapter you will know where value comes from and how to create value.

The Essence

Divine Microeconomy Model ©

Divine Microeconomy Model ©

This will be a model building experience for you. You may have never had an opportunity before to proceed step by step in an economic model to reach a coherent end. Additionally remarkable, this will be your chance to see firsthand how to build a bridge between science and religion. Take your time and enjoy the process.

To begin I need to extract the Divine Economy Model©, Diagram 2f from Chapter 2 in the book entitled MORE THAN LAISSEZ-FAIRE. The details about how that divine economy model was formed and developed was covered in the first chapter of this book.

Our starting point will be the same as Diagram 2f entitled "the complete Divine Economy Model independent of time."

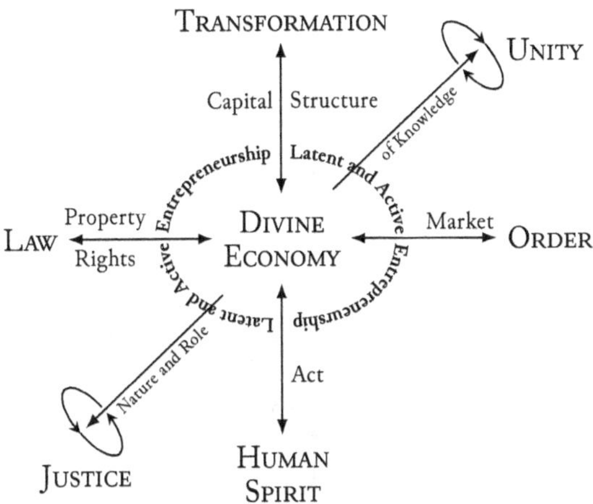

Diagram 2a: The complete Divine Economy Model independent of time

This is quite a complex and dynamic model in all of its applications but what we will take note of here, in particular, is that it is more than a two-dimensional model. I now call your attention to the description of the model; notably when the model was transformed from the "Modus Operandi" stage to the "Driving Force of the Divine Economy Model" stage in the process of the unfoldment of the Divine Economy Model ©. It is clear from the following description that it is more than a two-dimensional model: "The next modification of the divine economy model stretches the imagination a little by adding a depth dimension. This can be grasped fairly easily by imagining the modus operandi of the divine economy... as submerged in a bowl of water. The water that surrounds and supports the model represents latent and active entrepreneurship."

A more traditionally geometric way to see how the divine economy model takes on a higher-dimensional nature when there is the addition of the axis called "The Nature and Role of Knowledge." You are probably familiar with three-dimensional graphics which show what results from the addition of a z-axis to a two-dimensional graphic with an x- and a y-axis (Diagrams 2b and 2c).

In this case we will assume that the "Nature and Role of Knowledge"

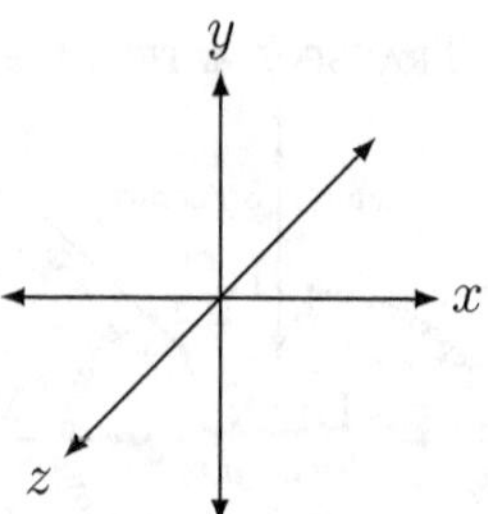

Diagram 2b: A standard three-dimensional figure

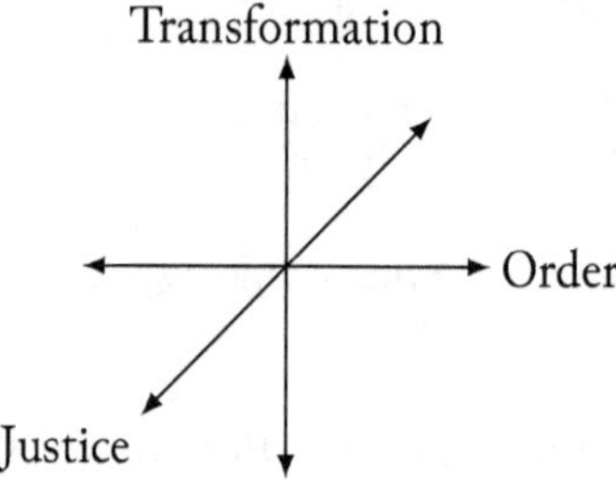

Diagram 2c: x, y, and z vectors of the Divine Economy Model

axis is the z-axis and imagine again that the three-dimensional model is submerged, immersed in a matrix of latent and active entrepreneurship.

We will now begin assessing the divine economy model from specific vantage points for the purpose of achieving the objective, which is to create the divine microeconomic model. The vantage points will be the end points of each of these principal vectors; x, y and z, looking toward the center of the model. The center of the model represents the equilibrating power which in this model is referred to as the 'divine economy.'

Looking toward the center from the vantage point of the end of one vector, opens a vista of a two-dimensional plane defined by the other two vectors (see Diagram 2d).

This two-dimensional plane can be seen not as different from planes that are very familiar to us such as a canvas of a painter, a tablet for verses, or a tapestry of fabric. Now is the best time to mention that all good science comes when science is artfully applied.

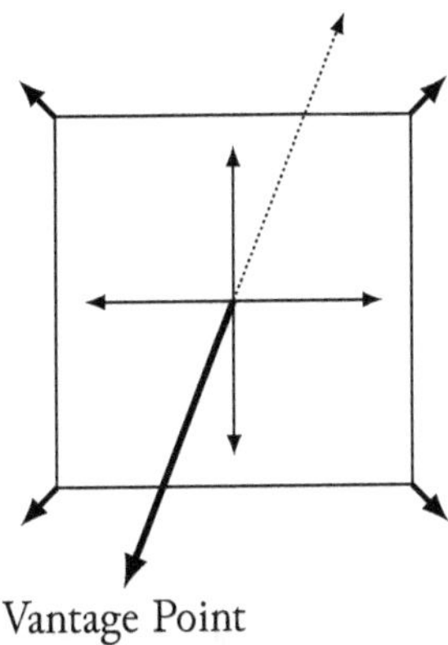

Diagram 2d: Vantage point view of the two-dimensional plane

The best in their fields of expertise are those who know both the art and the science of their profession and apply it wisely. This tapestry concept for the two-dimensional plane is a reminder that there is an art to the application of economic science.

I will now introduce the first stage—the Vantage Point Planes—of the divine microeconomy model. This first stage will show the model as a tapestry from a series of perspectives, as mentioned earlier; perspectives from the ends of each of the six vectors: $-x$, $+x$, $-y$, $+y$, $-z$, and $+z$.

The x-axis in the divine microeconomy model is represented by Law ($-x$) and Order ($+x$). The plane designation corresponds with the vantage point, so the Law/Order planes are seen in Diagram 2e.

The y-axis in the divine microeconomy model is represented by Human Spirit ($-y$) and Transformation ($+y$). The Human Spirit/Transformation planes are seen in Diagram 2f.

The z-axis in the divine microeconomy model is represented by Justice ($+z$) and Unity ($-z$). The Justice/Unity planes are seen in Diagram 2g.

Notice the pattern that I chose for labeling the planes, first one plane then the second one separated by a forward slash (e.g. Law/Order Plane). Although arbitrary to some extent, this naming pattern is motivated strongly by an understanding of cause and effect. Not in an absolute sense do things proceed in this manner but never-

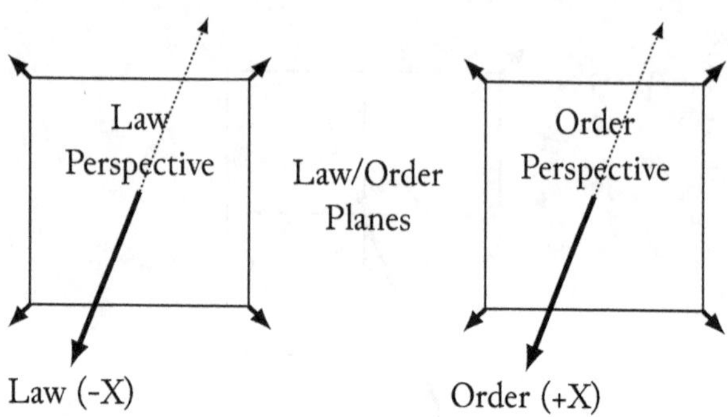

Diagram 2e: View of Law/Order planes

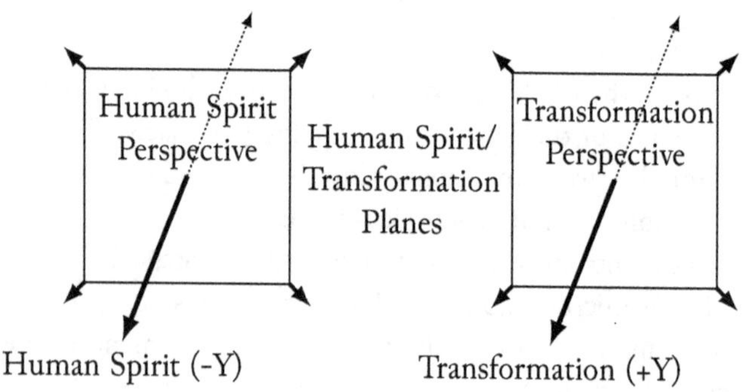

Diagram 2f: View of Human Spirit/Transformation planes

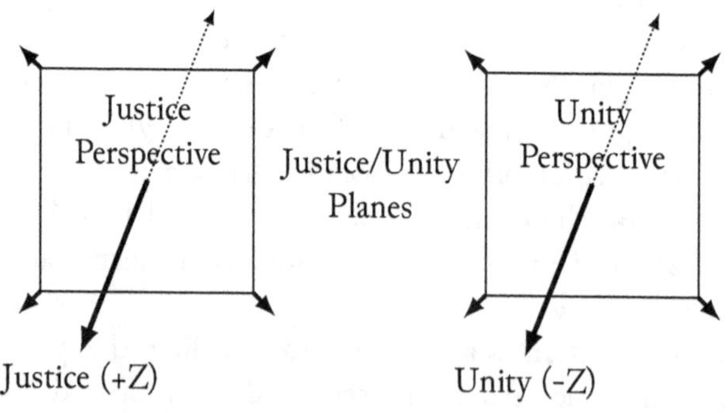

Diagram 2g: View of Justice/Unity planes

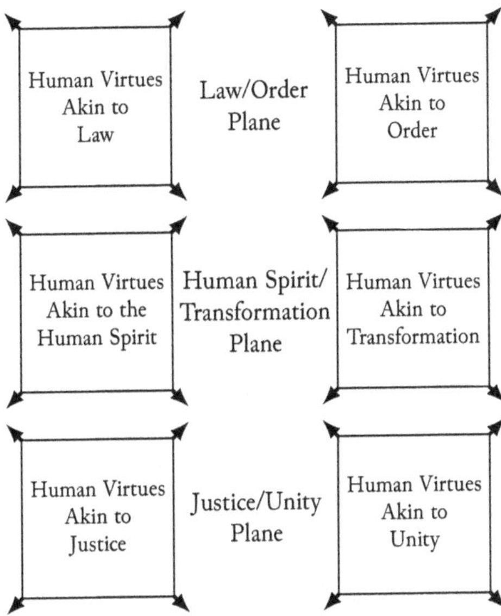

Diagram 2h: Virtues akin to the vantage point

theless there is a very real tendency for this pattern to be the dominant one. For example, if there is justice, unity can be established.

What is woven into the fabric of each of these tapestries? What is written upon these tablets? What is painted upon these canvases? The answer: human virtues!

The second stage of the divine microeconomy model, Virtues Akin to the Vantage Point, is gone into more detail in Chapter 4 of "Human Essence of Economics." Suffice it to say that all these planes are the seats of the human virtues akin to the name of the vantage point (Diagram 2h). For example, those virtues which reflect the ideal of unity reside on the Unity Plane.

The third and final stage of the divine microeconomy model, which is a divine microeconomic tapestry, incorporates two concepts that are deeply rooted in the human psyche (Diagram 2i). Our human logic and our understanding of the nature of the origin of things make these two concepts an essential part of human existence. One concept is cause and effect. The other concept is east and west. Both of these

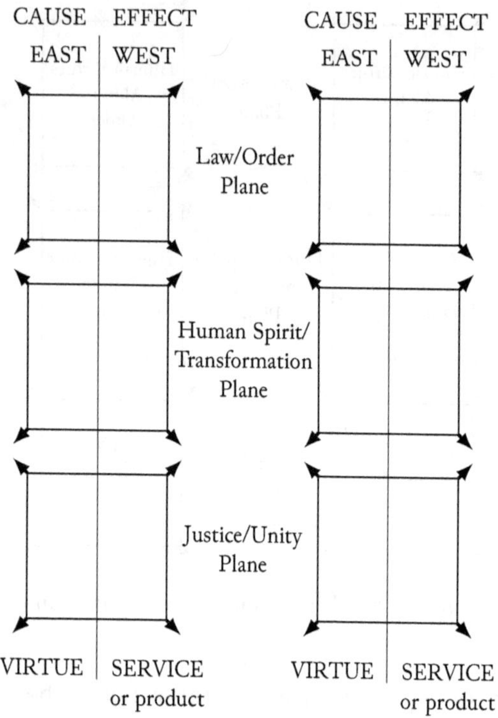

Diagram 2i: Divine Microeconomic Tapestry (also called the Divine Microeconomy Model©)

concepts appear to be strongly directional; from cause to effect, from east to west. However, the fact that new cycles can and do begin from the end-result shows an important degree of reciprocity.

Stage three introduces cause and effect, and east and west, by adding the element of service to the element of virtue. The symbolism of east and west is compatible with the cause and effect, producing the following pattern: virtue leading to service (or product) which then may stimulate a new cycle. The idea that the acquisition of a virtue (cause) leads to service or a product (effect), which may *inspire* a *desire* to *acquire* more virtue(s) or service, fits the purpose of this model.

Just like the Divine Economy Model©, this Divine Microeconomy Model© is a complex and dynamic model. Its symmetry and reciproc-

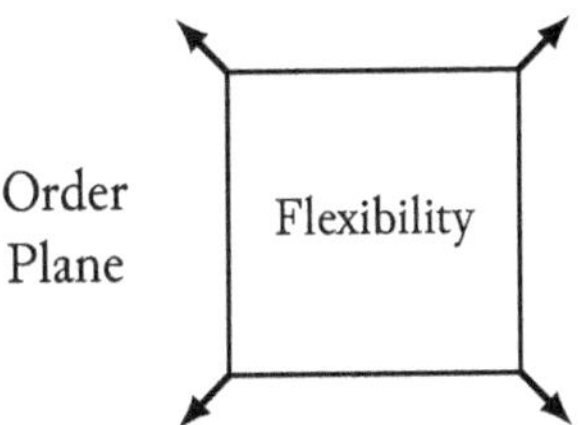

Virtue Illustration 1: 'Flexibility' in the Order plane

ity carry its essential simplicity forward, making practical applications of the model a real possibility. In essence this is a very powerful economic model!

The search after the source of value—virtues (ethics)—is the essence of the divine economy. Think of the divine economy as the means to the ends we've chosen. I will begin to exercise the Divine Microeconomy Model by selecting one virtue per vantage point plane and then I will systematically look at the economics taking place at the micro level, at the level of the individual.

Example One—'Flexibility' in the Order Plane

Each of us knows that having flexibility as a part of the order of things makes life much more enjoyable. Flexible order in our lives makes it easier for us to adjust to changes—the inevitable changes that occur in our lives.

Employers who provide an environment that incorporates flexibility will tend to have a 'happier' workforce that most likely will translate into a more productive and a more stable workforce. Also, customers appreciate having flexible and various options available to them if a product doesn't exactly meet their needs.

Flexibility incorporated into the production process—providing more options to employees and customers—leads to higher productivity and customer satisfaction, both of which are good for business.

Here we have customer satisfaction as one possible example of the 'tangible goods and services' emerging from flexibility.

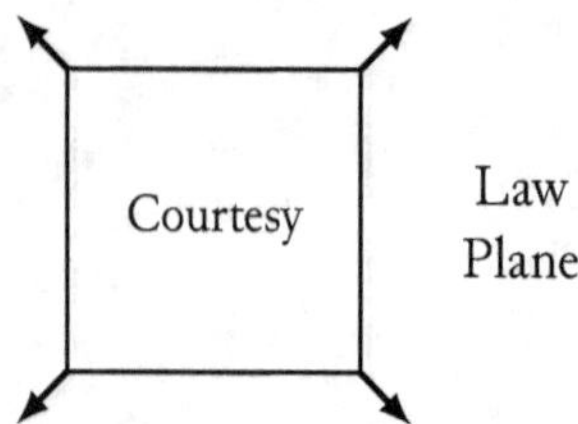

Virtue Illustration 2: 'Courtesy' in the Law plane

Example Two—'Courtesy' in the Law Plane

No one is offended by being treated with courtesy. It inspires greater respect for oneself and, most definitely, greater respect for the courteous person.

Since the market is the embodiment of social cooperation, courtesies become the norm. If it is courteous to be on time that becomes the standard, 'out of courtesy.' And each time these courteous practices are applied the social relationships advance to new levels of mutual respect. As a consequence cooperation and coordination improves.

Here we have market cooperation and coordination as examples of the 'tangible goods and services' emerging from courtesy. By acquiring and practicing courtesy, work relationships will change and there will be a tremendous increase in productivity since cooperation and coordination will increase.

Example Three—'Excellence' in the Human Spirit Plane

As an expression of my will to live and love life, I show a particular keenness towards the things that I enjoy. It follows, then, that I will continue to strive for excellence in that pursuit, whatever it is.

Matching the right task with the right person to perform the task is one key to productivity and entrepreneurs are alert to this prospect. If those who are producing a good or service excel at it then everyone in the entire economy benefits, ultimately.

Imagine yourself having to choose between various products of similar prices but you happen to know that one company has a reputation for excellent production standards. This attribute is known as product

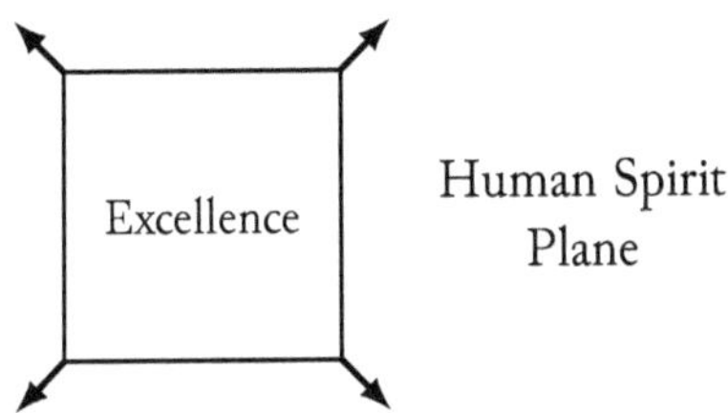

Virtue Illustration 3: 'Excellence' in the Human Spirit plane

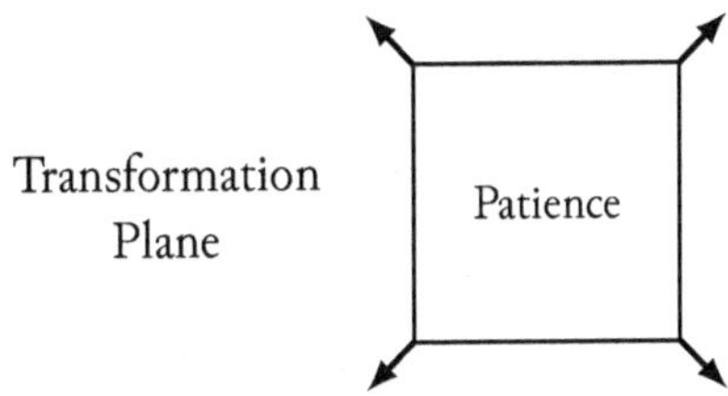

Virtue Illustration 4: 'Patience' in the Transformation plane

quality and it is a major factor in decision-making. Of course you, as well as everyone else, will choose the best product.

Here we have product quality as an example of the 'tangible goods and services' emerging from excellence. By acquiring and practicing excellence there will be a more refined division of labor which will translate into greater productivity.

Example Four—'Patience' in the Transformation Plane

There is no way that everything can be understood instantaneously. Processing and understanding takes time. Those who are patient are known for their wisdom, a wisdom that partially comes from the practice of patience.

The same is true for production. It takes time. The goods and services that people want need to be generated and those who can envision and nurture the production process patiently over time render a great service.

Everyone can participate in this patience-requiring production process by exercising patience themselves—exhibited in their lives

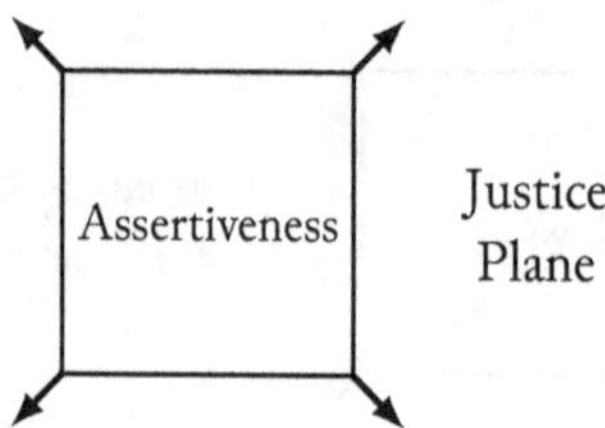

Virtue Illustration 5: 'Assertiveness' in the Justice plane

by saving. This saving and investment then converts into the much needed capital used in production processes, which can be seen as the economic equivalent to patience since capital represents goods for the future.

Here we have capital as an example of the 'tangible goods and services' emerging from patience. By acquiring and practicing patience, errors from short-sighted decisions will decrease and the savings necessary for economic growth will more likely be available.

Example Five—'Assertiveness' in the Justice Plane

Nobody can read your mind. If you take it upon yourself to make sure that others know what is important to you, then you can claim to be assertive.

The market is a dynamic process and it requires some assertive behavior to function properly. The alert entrepreneurs are actually assertive about the discrepancies that they find and they are assertive in applying their subsequent action.

It is this dispersal of knowledge that results from the actions taken by the entrepreneurs that keeps the whole system working and keeps knowledge flowing. Assertive and active entrepreneurs are, therefore, major contributors to the elimination of ignorance.

Here we have entrepreneurship as an example of the 'tangible goods and services' emerging from assertiveness. By acquiring and practicing assertiveness the speed and accuracy of the flow of knowledge will improve, leading to the discovery of more opportunities.

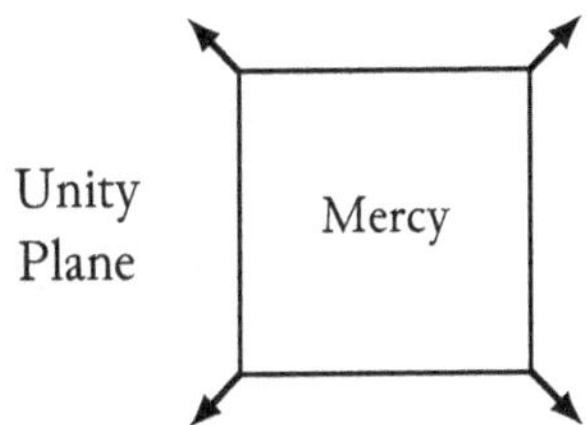

Virtue Illustration 6: 'Mercy' in the Unity plane

Example Six—'Mercy' in the Unity Plane

The world is a testing ground for our souls. Tests and difficulties exist and have to be dealt with.

How can we truly show that we care without a capacity for mercy? Those who feel blessed in plenteousness often show their feelings of mercy by contributing to or participating in some kind of charity. Charities channel peoples' mercy to those in need.

Mercy is one of the keys to prosperity. It is through the act of being merciful that one begins and continues to recognize the reasons to be thankful, and the act of being merciful also makes one feel prosperous. It is through mercy that those who are suffering are given their much needed sustenance which, too, is a prosperous feeling indeed.

Here we have the feeling of prosperity as an example of the 'tangible goods and services' emerging from mercy. By acquiring and practicing mercy the extremes of wealth and poverty will lessen and a greater sense of prosperity will be felt by all. Those who show mercy will be recognized for this noble and valuable trait. A price, a 'premium' in some form, can be ascribed to the practice of 'mercy', i.e., there is a commercial aspect to the virtue. It is a traceable market phenomenon.

Statement: Now you know where value comes from, and how to create value.

See What Happens When You Take These Action Steps:

- Be a producer so you have sources of income.
- Be alert to what, when, where, and how people find value.

- Most likely you will have many roles to play; as an entrepreneur, as a skilled laborer, as a capitalist, as an owner of resources. Learn to master them.
- Cooperate with others to accomplish goals.

Want to see how this extends into ethical economics? See Chapter 3.

Chapter 3

Envisioning Your Path*

Calibrating your moral compass in a confusing world is one of your aspirations. The rich experiences you've had so far in your life have made you wiser and more perceptive. Your sincere quest to find your bearings is not something to be taken lightly. What becomes clearer and clearer to you is that the path you are on is leading you in a direction that fulfills your dreams.

Succumbing to the moral relativity of the age we live in is something we seemingly all have in common. It is all around us and it misdirects us and scatters our focus. It also weakens us to the point where we become apathetic about the value of having true bearings. We all are struggling with that.

Rest assured there is substance and there is a foundation that supports and sustains us at all times. The economy is providential, and it is built upon virtues and service. It has within it everything that is needed for everyone to flourish together. It is a powerful means of transformation.

A major cause of the confusion in this age of moral relativity is the separation of ethics and economics and the proclaimed inability to bridge them together. This lack of progress is to blame for our dilemma. There is a strange inertia that exists only because we are being held hostage by those with poor scientific inquiry and by those with little trust in the excellence of human moral reason.

Advocates of moral relativity believe that needed changes will alter the very core of human reality. This intentional disarrangement is a rotten fruit that leads to chaos and annihilation of human well-being. There is a balance between reason and faith yet the advocates of moral

*This is an excerpt from Chapter 3 of my book "Ethical Economics for Today and Tomorrow".

relativity attack this balance and work to undermine both reason and faith.

Now you will see the flash of a different spark that when it comes into contact with kindling, the kindling of minds that are searching for ethical economics, will catch fire and turn into a blaze:

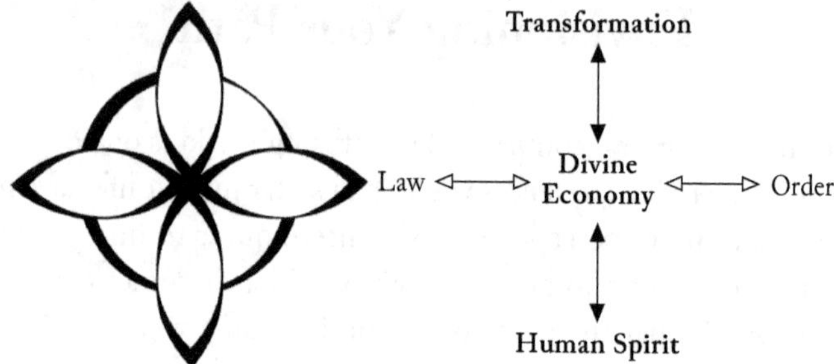

The journey must begin. The ship needs to be constructed and it needs to be launched. Navigation toward your destination is required. This cannot be done for you although some are trying to do just that. You are the constructor and navigator of the ship and so, captain, use it to take you to your destination.

Building the Ship

Model of the Ethics of the Divine Economy ©

Concept of the Divine Economy

Many observers over the years have noticed the natural tendency of human beings to associate and cooperate, benefiting (changing) from this interaction. A question arises: What is the nature of the forces that bring about these changes?

Not long ago I began to contemplate and conceptualize about the forces at work. I refused to separate human action from human reality. In my mind I perceived, and then preserved, the divine station of human creation and made it into an inviolable identity in the broad concept of the divine economy.

The station of 'created in His Image' implies that each individual has the potential to be the focal point, the point of action which energizes

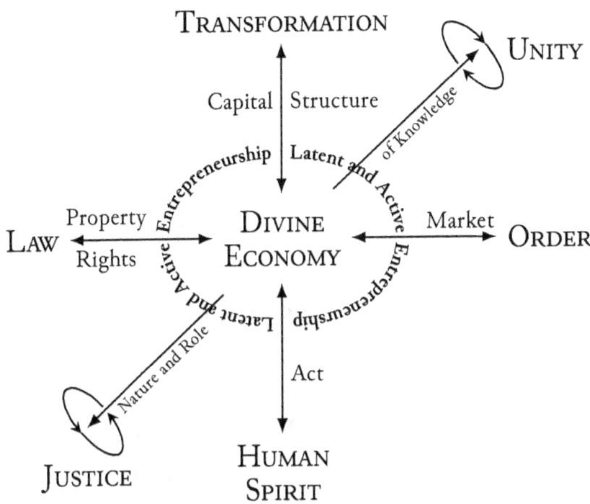

Diagram 3a: The Complete Divine Economy Model

the surrounding world. And so relative to each human being (whom also has the nature to be social) the economy manifests itself.

I now refer you to the Complete Divine Economy Model© which was published in my first book in 2015.

This model is an original and significant contribution to economic science. Its significance is growing. The reason is because it is capable of taking economics to new horizons.

One of the most notable outcomes of this model is the identification of the center of the model as the 'divine economy'. The center represents the force behind it all. In economic terms the center is the force behind the tendencies of equilibrium.

Another outcome has to do with the third axis which is called the 'Nature and Role of Knowledge.' Since that axis also goes directly through the center—the divine economy—it serves its purpose best when it is in its pure form. Unfortunately it is subject to disruption and corruption if there is human intervention. Human understanding is, simply stated, finite and not capable of fully comprehending the divine, and so, intervention (imposition of a finite and limited understanding of reality) always creates an injustice.

In summary, the economy is a divine institution that is a part of the human creation as a whole. By way of the divine economy the grace and bounty of God flows with abundance and justice whereas human intervention can hamper and has hampered that flow. Nevertheless it is important to know that the essence of the human creation, each of us individually and also our association as social creatures, is divine in nature.

And so there is now a new definition of economic equilibrium. It is referred to as the divine economy. Upon it is hoisted a new mantle, the mantle of 'moral authority.' The unhampered economy allows the will of man to align itself with the Will of God. But is there a way to confirm this assertion? Yes.

I now refer you to the Divine Microeconomy Model© which was introduced in my second book, published in 2015 (Diagram 3b).

This model did what had never been done before—it built a bridge between economic science and religion! Needless to say this is of great significance to the scientific discipline of ethics.

Clearly there is much overlap between ethics and virtues. To a very large extent they are interchangeable. What I discovered as I extended the divine economy theory to the microlevel was that the appearance of these 'names of God' (that is, the virtues embodied in some form) is what attracts human beings (Diagram 3c).

In economics the things that people want are called goods. We also know with certainty that virtues are goods, not bads. So underlying all economic goods and services, what makes them goods, is the manifestation of virtues in them in some form.

The great discovery made in THE HUMAN ESSENCE OF ECONOMICS is that the origin of all value is the appearance of the 'names of God'—the virtues. This causes a direct link to ethics and so for divine economy theory to advance further a model of the ethics of the divine economy was necessary. This is why I began this endeavor. And this is how.

Concept of the Model of the Ethics of the Divine Economy

A model that depicts the ethics of the divine economy has to acknowledge the existence of God! Needless to say, atheism is completely refuted as a silly and destructive notion. Everything, visible and invisible, is proof of the existence of God.

There are relationships and symbols throughout creation that are

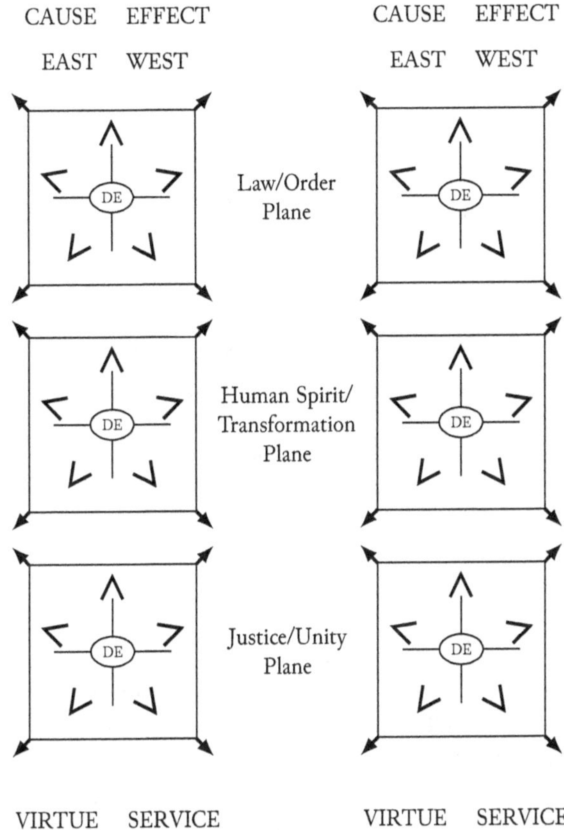

Diagram 3b: Divine Microeconomy Model with the Divine Economy Spark

fully recognized by the human intellect and which make the infinite more approachable by the finite. An example of one such relationship is a covenant. There is power that comes from a covenant, which is a type of contract. A question arises: How can a simple promise or agreement generate such power?

Continuing along these lines, another example of a symbol which makes the infinite more approachable for the finite mind is an axis. An axis represents a force and power far greater than just a pivot round which something rotates. It takes on the possibilities of infinity because of its design pattern—it extends to infinity in both directions

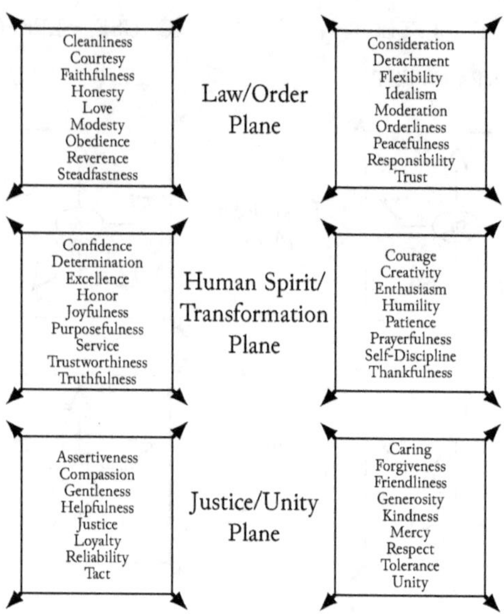

Diagram 3c: Six Planes and Fifty-Two Virtues

and it is capable of rotating at infinite speeds—and it empowers the human mind to stretch and grasp reality much farther.

To begin the ethics model, I focus attention on the Human Spirit/Transformation axis (vertical) of the Divine Economy Model © (refer back to Diagram 3a). Therefore notice the dimming of the Law/Order (horizontal) axis (Diagram 3d).

Like the relationships and symbols I just mentioned, this representation is infinitely complex even though it is a simple diagram. Imagine now how and where human virtues fit in.

As the human spirit searches for and acquires virtues; transformation takes place. As the virtues already acquired are refined and perfected; transformation takes place. The divine economy—where the flow of the knowledge of the aspirations of all humans on the planet takes place—is the discovery and testing ground for the virtues.

In search for virtues, in search for an ethic, we use all of the intellectual tools at our disposal. Language, specifically written language, is one of these major tools. There is no doubt that the Scriptures, the Holy Books, serve as a repository of knowledge about virtues. These

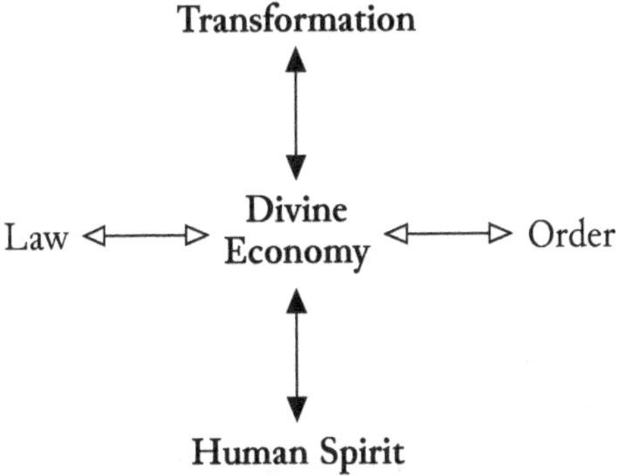

Diagram 3d: Ethics Aspect of the Divine Economy Model

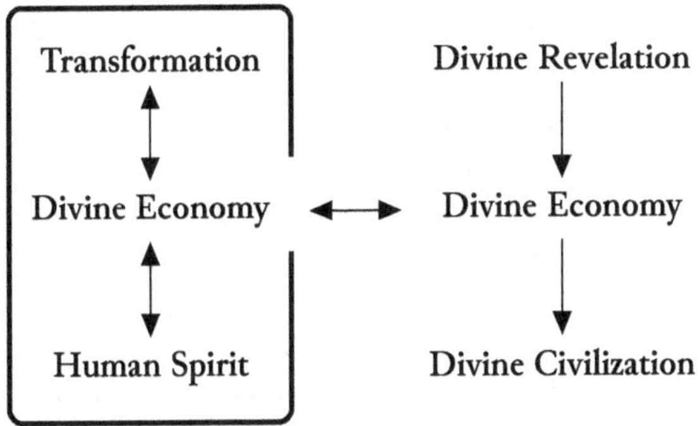

Diagram 3e: Model of the Ethics of the Divine Economy

Holy Books, as far as their origin is concerned, are considered Revelation from God. The content in the Holy Books that is directly attributed to the Voice of God is referred to as the Word of God.

I now return to the concept of a covenant, we find that in the Scriptures, God enters into a covenant with those 'created in His Image.' The covenant states that He would never leave them to themselves; He would never deprive them of His love and grace.

This concept allows me to add the second component of the ethics model of the divine economy (Diagram 3e).

The potential outcome of each Revelation is the appearance of a divine civilization; of course, relative to the spiritual and social capacity of humankind for that dispensation.

Notice in the diagram the role played by the divine economy. It not only serves as the discovery and testing ground for the virtues but it also is the means for the attainment of the divine civilization!

Attention is needed here. The search after virtues, ethics, is the essence of the divine economy and the divine economy is the means to the ends. It is therefore not possible to advance economic theory without advancing ethical theory.

To conclude this section I introduce the shorthand designation for the model of the ethics of the divine economy. It is DR/DE/DC, short for Divine Revelation/Divine Economy/Divine Civilization.

Symbolism of the Model of the Ethics of the Divine Economy

This model has merit in its simplicity—DR/DE/DC—and in its complexity. It is not an easy task—developing a model that represents historical, scientific and spiritual truths!

We are not finished with the very powerful concept of the Covenant of God. What is the other half, the reciprocal half of that covenant? God promises to guide us; but what is our end of the deal? Reciprocally we are bound together as one human family. Perhaps that is the underlying reason why we are basically social creatures. Nevertheless, the economy is the divine institution that enables us to fulfill our end of the deal.

The Divine Microeconomy Model© (refer back to Diagram 3b) accomplishes the remarkable feat of bridging economic science and religion. One consequence of that model is that the simplicity of the essence of economics is identified as the appearance of virtues in ourselves and others and in what we produce. This is what is valued.

To further develop the ethics model I continue the application of the concept of the covenant. This time the model is placed in juxtaposition to a portion of the symbol of the 'Greatest Name' which was designed by ʿAbduʾl-Bahá (Diagram 3f).

Although in the original language of Arabic this symbol is actually letters composing a name it also is a symbol of reality. Let me describe the symbol for you. Notice that the top horizontal line and bottom horizontal line look alike. The top represents God and the bottom represents the human being 'created in His Image.'

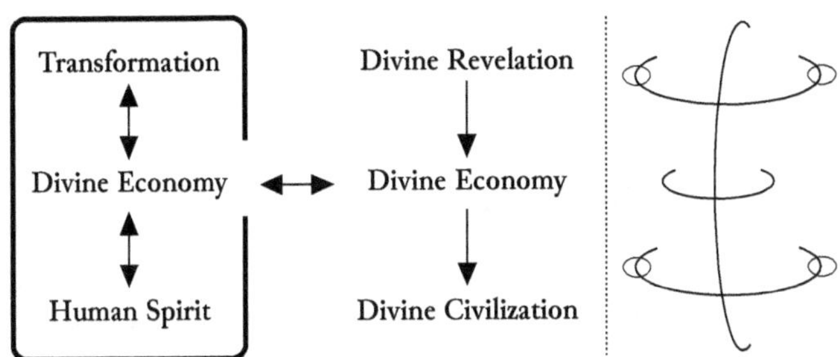

Diagram 3f: Complete Model of the Ethics of the Divine Economy

The center horizontal line represents the Manifestations of God, sent in every age to guide and educate humanity as promised as part of the Covenant. The center vertical line represents the Holy Spirit, the Word of God, which connects finite humans to the infinite God and teaches us His Will.

The reason I placed the 'Greatest Name' symbol in juxtaposition to the model is to make some comparisons and to contrast. This exercise is an example of combining both the art and science of economics. You are about to experience the beauty (the quality of a thought that arouses admiration or approval) of this scientific model.

Pause for a moment in comparison. Notice the horizontal layers across all three representations; and notice the similarities in what they represent. Now compare how in each form there is also a verticality to them which seems to bring together realms that otherwise might be perceived as unconnected.

Changing to a contrasting mode also reveals some very exciting points of beauty. The vertical connecting symbol in the 'Greatest Name' is continuous; ever-flowing as promised in the covenant.

Whereas if you notice in the Complete Model of the Ethics of the Divine Economy (Diagram 3f)—in the portion brought over from Diagram 3e—in the leftmost portion the vertical movement needs to 'enter and exit,' flowing in both directions and undergoing some kind of processing along the way. And then notice that in the rightmost portion of the model, (DR/DE/DC) brought over from Diagram 3e, the flow is only unidirectional.

The main benefit from juxtaposing the 'Greatest Name' with the

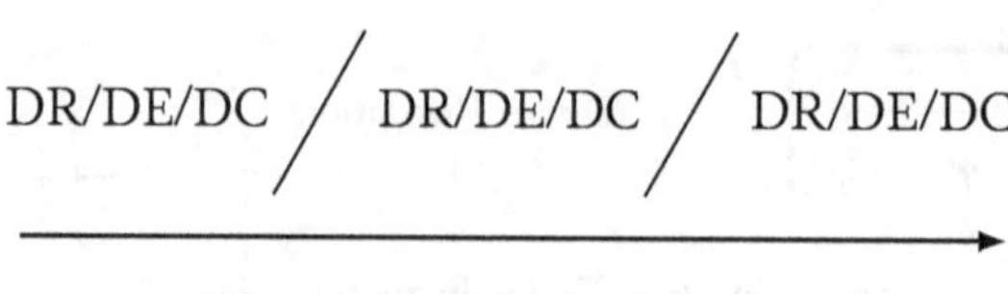

Diagram 3g: Change Over Time

model in Diagram 3e was to gain a further understanding of the moral authority of the divine economy. There is a sacredness in this covenant between God and each of us. The divine economy is part of the fulfillment of our sacred nature, that is, our 'created in His Image' nature.

Cyclical Nature of the Model of the Ethics of the Divine Economy

What we see as a cycle in the divine microeconomy is this: 1) the discovery of virtue(s) in the divine economy matrix (also referred to as the market process), 2) followed by the acquisition of virtue(s) in some form, 3) and then transformation, which only serves to sharpen the discerning powers. This leads to more discoveries of those things that we inherently value, whether they appear as material goods or as 'ideal' goods.

In the ethics model, the unidirectional portion of the DR/DE/DC model (the right half of Diagram 3e) appears to exhibit finality but that is a 'short-run' phenomenon. Within a single dispensation there is a fully completed cycle which comes to an end. In the long run the model would have a more dynamic nature as represented in Diagram 3g.

The determining factors of these cycles since the beginning of time have been the condition of the world; that is, the physical, intellectual, and spiritual evolution of humanity.

This is part of what is called the Greater Covenant of God. When human beings are ready to receive the next Revelation then it occurs. This can be represented by the following diagram.

It is clear from Diagram 3h that the Model of the Ethics of the Divine Economy© has a cyclical nature. Viewed from this broad perspective it becomes clear and evident that the divine economy is the means to attain the ends over and over again. It is also clear and evident that the divine economy can be viewed in terms of cause and

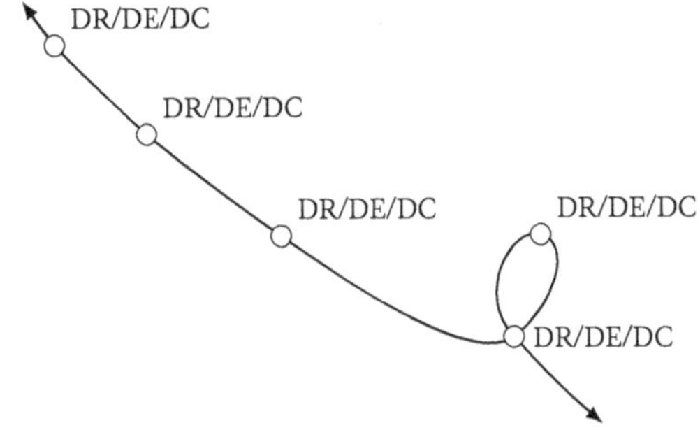

Diagram 3h: Cyclical Nature of the Model of the Ethics of the Divine Economy

effect. In other words, the divine economy theory is causal-realistic. There is a cause and effect relationship between the divine economy and the divine civilization.

Economics is the study of the means to attain ends and that is exactly why the divine economy theory is so important. The divine economy is the means! Therefore, it is to be studied.

Equally as monumental a finding is the inseparability of economics and ethics. What is evident beyond question is that the Manifestations of God are the true, real, and original Ethicists. Equally true: the Word of God revealed by the Manifestations of God is the foundation of ethics. Let's give honor to where it is due—God is our Creator and He is the Source of all knowledge.

Statement: Now you are better able to navigate your ship to reach your destination.

See What Happens When You Take These Action Steps:

- Be more conscious of the virtues that underlie all value.
- Socially cooperate and notice the signals in the market.
- Be an agent of the market process by being alert, by taking calculated risks, and by distributing and preserving capital.
- Be confident that your ethical decisions are also economic decisions.

Want to see how this extends into economic justice? See Chapter 4.

Chapter 4

Seeing How You Fit In*

What you do has merit. Regardless of any of your physical characteristics, you possess the inherent power to bring value into existence in unique ways. And you are the sovereign of your contributions. That is your domain. The unique gift that you offer is in harmony with all that is going on in the world since the world is for us and our job is to apply our gift in a balanced way.

When the scales are tipped the outcomes do not necessarily reflect the quality of the input. Imbalances caused by the obstructionists, the interventionists, skew the affairs of the world and often that means that your endeavor goes unnoticed. It's no wonder you feel underappreciated, invisible.

The economy is providential once the forces of equilibrium are released from the chains of interventionism. One of the best ways to free it is for us to recognize our sovereignty, both as buyers and as producers. Our domain starts with us, our mind and heart, and extends peacefully via voluntary social cooperation as far as you and I can reach.

No doubt the advocates of the top-down system that is in place will use whatever means at their disposal to discourage or even squash the ideas of individual sovereignty and voluntary social cooperation. Their clamor will insist that we need to be cared for by the 'experts' and the wise 'leaders' or else all things will fall apart! What is going to fall apart is their system because it cannot withstand the power of economic equilibrium.

Any and all efforts to constrain economic equilibrium are futile and

*This is an excerpt from Chapter 3 of my book "Liberty & Justice of Economic Equilibrium".

immoral. We are the victims of this injustice but finally there is a fully integrated economic theory that eradicates statism. It is the nature of economic equilibrium to bring into balance justice and liberty. The advocates of the top-down system and those who propagate false economic beliefs to prop that system up have no moral authority and they have no economic reasoning to justify their system.

Now you will see the flash of a different spark that when it comes into contact with kindling, the kindling of minds searching for economic justice, will catch fire and turn into a blaze:

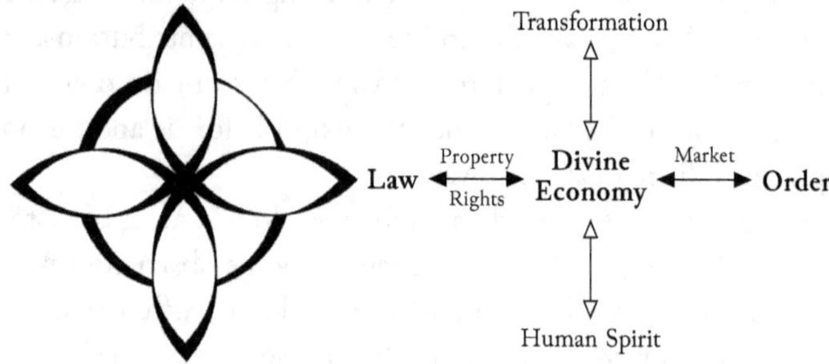

A New Perspective

The Economic Justice Model

Incubation

"Each individual is the only and final arbiter in matters concerning his own satisfaction and happiness." This quote by Ludwig von Mises summarizes the concept of liberty and justice very well. My job in this chapter is to further elucidate this theme in a cohesive way such that the literature of classical liberalism and the work I have done on the macro, micro, and ethical economics of the divine economy are all brought together. Mises says, "No science can avoid abstract concepts, and he who abhors them should stay away from science and see whether and how he can go through life without them."

We start with the perfectly proportioned concept of a circle to represent economic equilibrium which is also referred to as the divine economy (Diagram 3a).

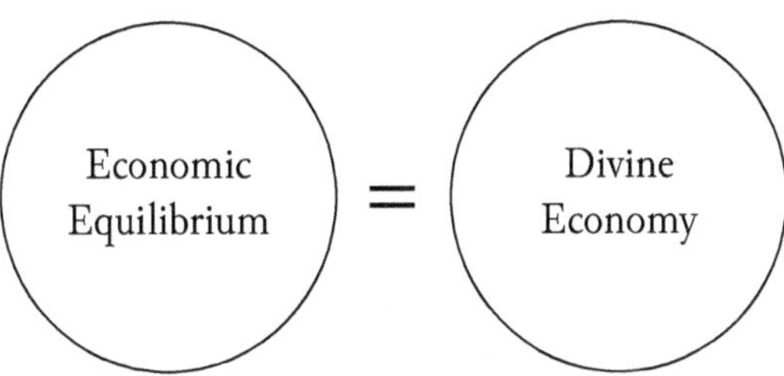

Diagram 3a: Divine Economy Theory Identity

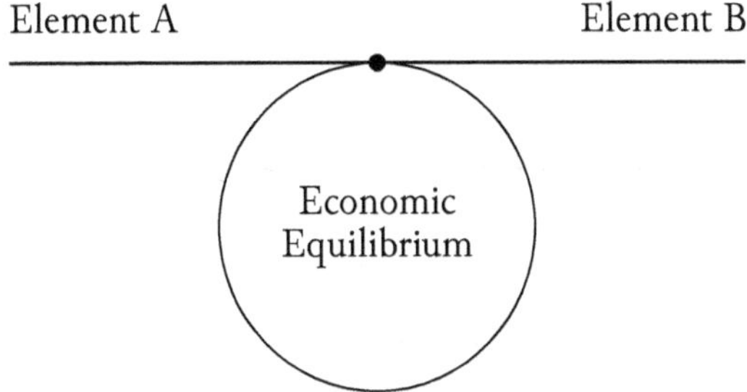

Diagram 3b: Interface of Divine Economy with the Elements of Human Civilization

How does this circle come in contact with other elements of human civilization in a two-dimensional graphic representation? It is either intersected or it comes in contact at the tangent (Diagram 3b).

Tangency represents the single and therefore pure relationship between the circle (equilibrium) and the element.

In a sense there is a balance at that single point. Another way to represent the idea of balance would be to show the elements of human civilization teetering on a fulcrum as shown in Diagram 3c.

This is the starting point for our analysis of the liberty and justice of economic equilibrium (Diagram 3d).

We will return to this progression of steps at the end of this chapter.

The model being developed in this chapter is the fourth in a sequence of four. The first model, laid out in detail in More Than Laissez-Faire, was the macroeconomic model (Diagram 3e):

Implied in the model is my redefinition of praxeology as the study

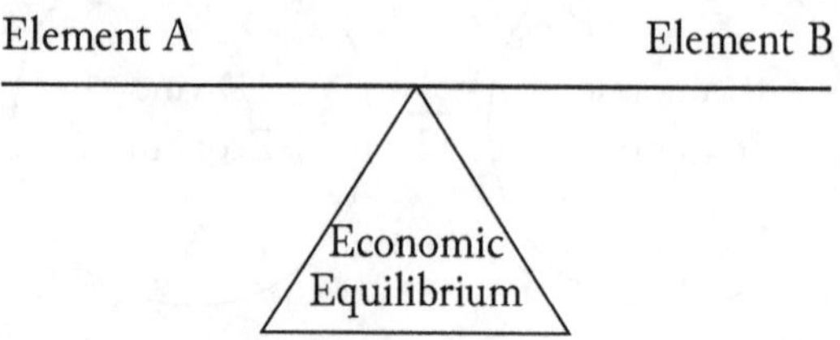

Diagram 3c: The Divine Economy Fulcrum

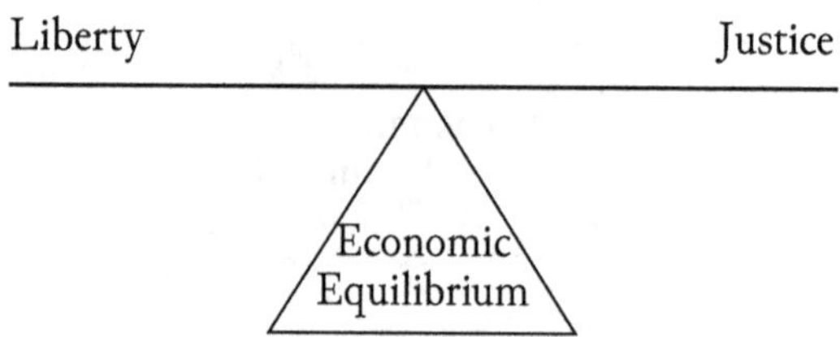

Diagram 3d: The Liberty and Justice of the Divine Economy

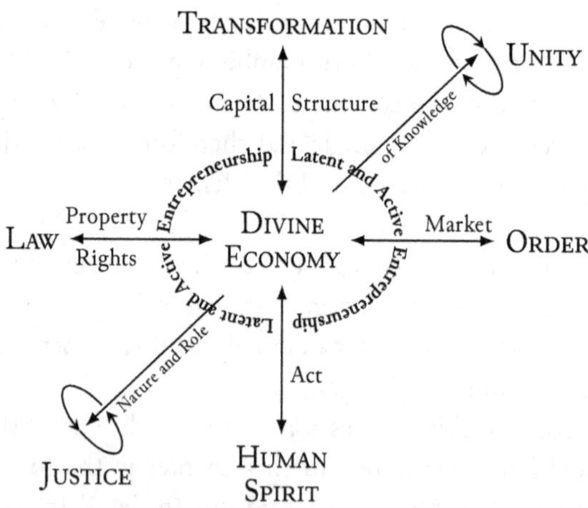

Diagram 3e: The Complete Divine Economy Model

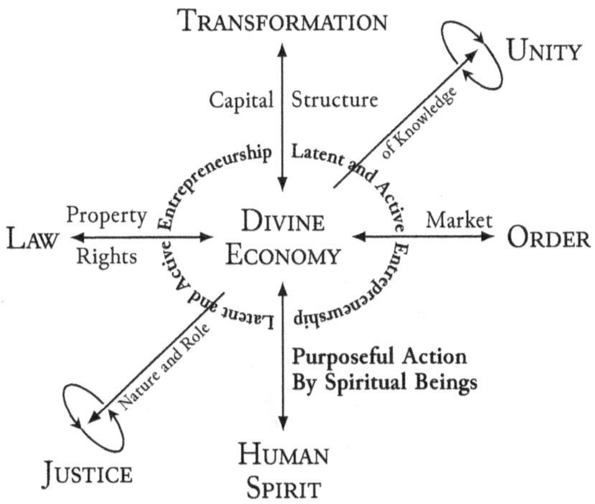

Diagram 3f: The Model with New Definition of Praxeology

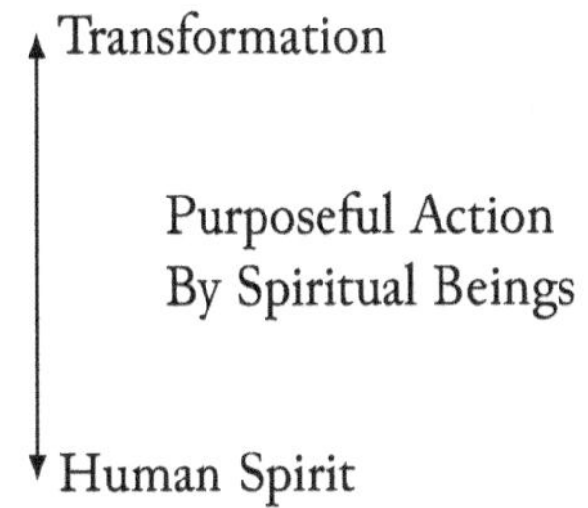

Diagram 3g: We'll Call It the Human Reality

of purposeful action by spiritual beings. Since this redefinition is of major significance I altered the model to highlight the importance of this redefinition (Diagram 3f).

The implication, then, is that the act itself is divine (in other words, performed by a spiritual being) which adds great meaning to the simple, central, vertical, Human Spirit/Transformation portion of the model (Diagram 3g). In a sense, it simply and profoundly represents the human reality.

The macro model is dynamic, not static, and so to represent changes over time we have Diagram 3h.

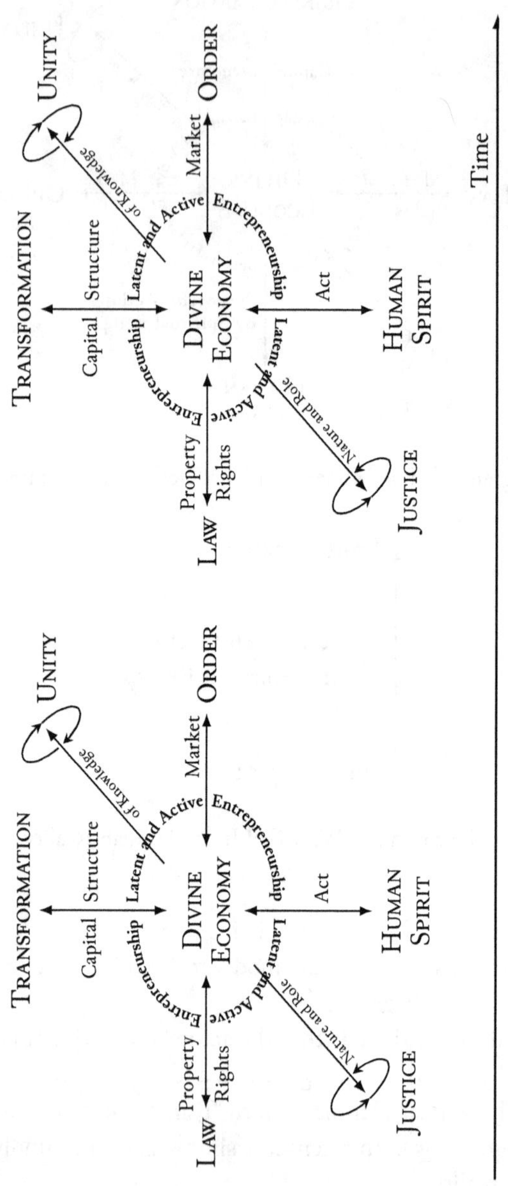

Diagram 3h: The Complete Divine Economy Model Over Time

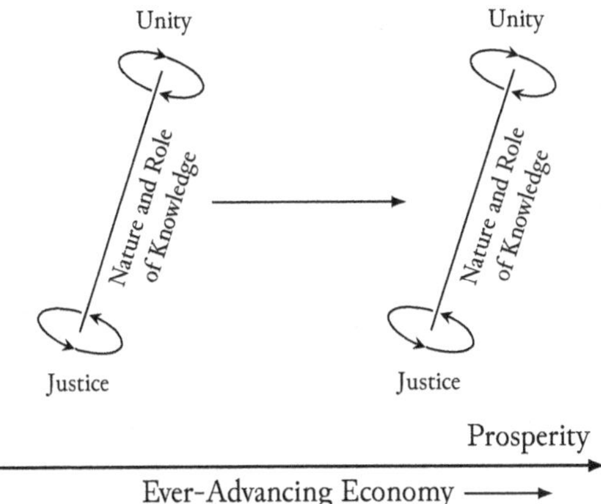

Diagram 3i: Shorthand Version of the Divine Economy Model Over Time

As a shorthand method of representing this movement we just show the movement of the Nature and Role of Knowledge axis (Diagram 3i), which importantly gives emphasis to the nature and role of knowledge in a human civilization.

Here is an interesting quote of Ludwig von Mises: "Metaphysics and theology are not, as the positivists pretend, products of an activity unworthy of Homo sapiens, remnants of mankind's primitive age that civilized people ought to discard. They are a manifestation of man's unappeasable craving for knowledge." Especially important for us to consider now is this movement of the Justice/Unity axis, which is another name for this axis. It can also be regarded as the axis of the oneness of the world of humanity.

Let's step back. Economics is the science of the study of the means to attain ends. Along these lines I am now going to suggest that we take a slightly different perspective when looking at the complete model given in Diagram 3e. Further developing the ideas given in Diagram 3f and in Diagram 3g and applying this new definition of praxeology, I found another gem in the model. With all of this in mind, while looking at Diagram 3f imagine that the Human Spirit/Transformation (vertical) axis represents the human reality; in other words, it captures the essence of what we are and what we are doing. The Law/Order (horizontal) axis represents the means, that is, what we have to have for us to get where we are going (law and order, respectively). And finally the Justice/Unity axis represents the ends, what it is that we want (justice and unity, respectively).

As soon as we talk about ends we enter into the realm of ethics but since ethics and economics are inseparable they can both be explored and examined at the same time scientifically. Ends and means are not discretely or absolutely distinct, nor are they independent, so we need to use logic and curiosity to advance our understanding. Means and ends can and do morph into each other to some extent.

Tabernacle

Continuing along these lines let's consider another perspective. Humans use means to attain ends. In other words Human Spirit/Transformation (human reality) uses Law (means) to bring about Order (ends). And Human Spirit/Transformation (human reality) uses Justice (means) to bring about Unity (ends). The ultimate end which is composed of Order and Unity is social cooperation, which is also a means, as identified by Henry Hazlitt in THE FOUNDATIONS OF MORALITY.

Freeing ourselves up to investigate at the same time both ethics (ends) and economics (means) makes sense since they are intertwined in the real world. Unless unshackled from the restrictions mandated by orthodoxy—noticeably so prior to the emergence of divine economy theory—then many fruits will be left undiscovered.

The Nature and Role of Knowledge axis is quite fascinating. It is a vector that extends to infinity in both directions indicating that there is not and never will be a scarcity of knowledge. Once placed in the model it intersects and interacts with the innumerable means of the real world (Diagram 3j)!

Imagine this axis spinning at phenomenal rates so as to accommodate the transference of information at lightning speed (the internet, for example). "The nature of a scarce resource is that use by one person excludes use by another; but you don't need to own the information that guides your action in order to have successful action. For example, two people can make a cake at the same time. They each have to

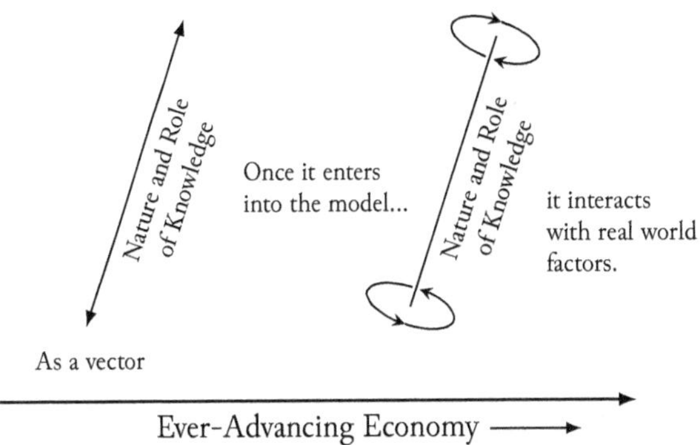

Diagram 3j: The Spinning Knowledge Vector

have their own ingredients, but they can use the same recipe at the same time. Material progress is made over time in human society because information is not scarce. It can be infinitely multiplied, learned, taught, and built on. The more patterns, recipes, causal laws that are known add to the stock of knowledge available to all actors and act as a greater and greater wealth multiplier by allowing actors to engage in ever-more efficient and productive actions. It is a good thing that ideas are infinitely reproducible, not a bad thing. There is no need to impose artificial scarcity on these things to make them more like scarce resources, which, unfortunately, are scarce. Knowledge is power because it guides action. It opens up a wider, richer universe of possibilities: it allows human actors to choose from a wider array of ends, and from a wider, richer set of means to achieve one's preferred ends."

In the context of the means/ends conversation what we have is: knowledge + means potentially leads to the attainment of ends. This is the ever-present economic problem! The solution to the problem is inherently a part of the divine economy—purposeful human action. How can I best describe the catalyst of the process—the driving force that is hidden underneath the solution? Entrepreneurship! Entrepreneurs are visionaries that cause the Justice/Unity axis to move to the right (Diagram 3k).

Whoosh! Now we have entered into the divine microeconomy. The entrepreneur is the one who is alert. He or she is alert to the new (mingled with the old) knowledge and is alert to the scarcity of resources.

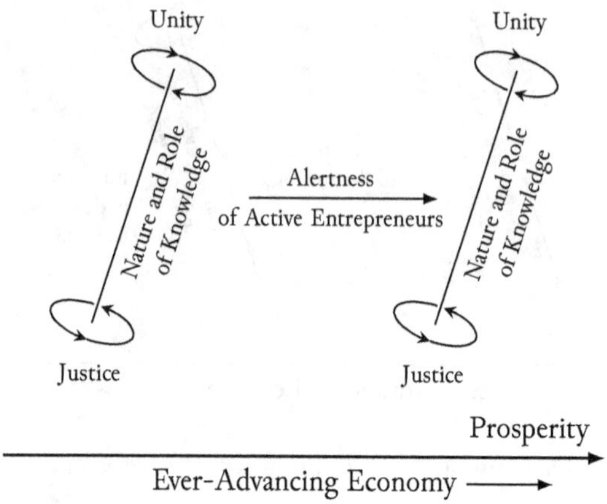

Diagram 3k: Entrepreneurs as the Driving Force

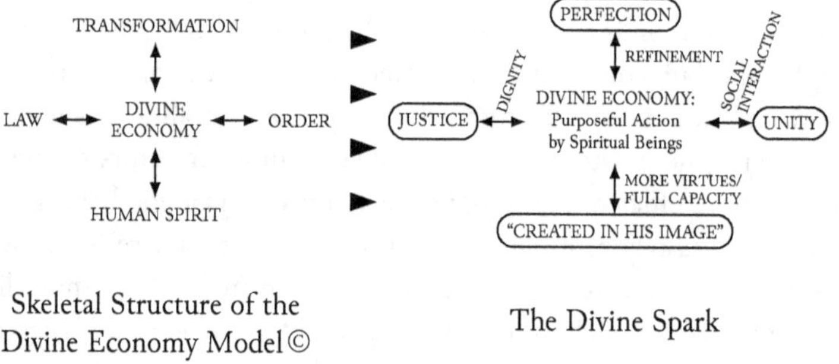

Diagram 3l: The Divine Spark and Its Derivation

As I described in THE HUMAN ESSENCE OF ECONOMICS all humans are entrepreneurs, either latent or active, and those that are active have ignited the divine spark as shown in Diagram 3l.

Then I introduced the shorthand version of the divine spark which displayed a radial symmetry and then, next, the divine spark was fully incorporated into (the second model of the sequence of four) the Complete Divine Microeconomy Model (Diagram 3m).

Alertness is another way of saying 'seeking after truth.' It certainly has an intellectual component but it also has a spiritual component

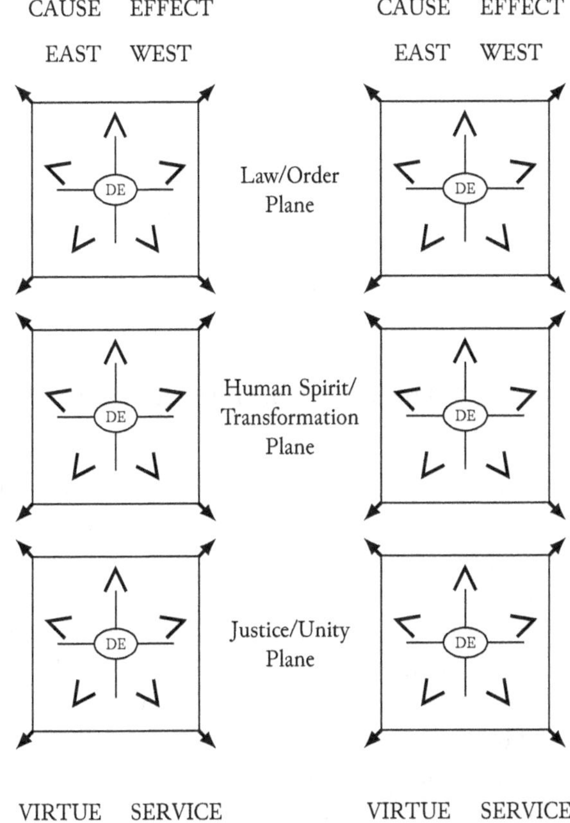

Diagram 3m: The Complete Divine Microeconomy Model

which has been unnecessarily neglected by those scientists that are still shackled to some extent by orthodoxy. The seat of all value is the appearance of the virtues or attributes of God in all material things and as the essential component of all human action. It is the appearance of these virtues, and the attraction that they create, that brings about both justice and unity.

First of all, since we are investigating justice let's go ahead and consider justice at the point of the ignition of the divine spark. Alertness of the entrepreneur is the exercising of the most basic human right,

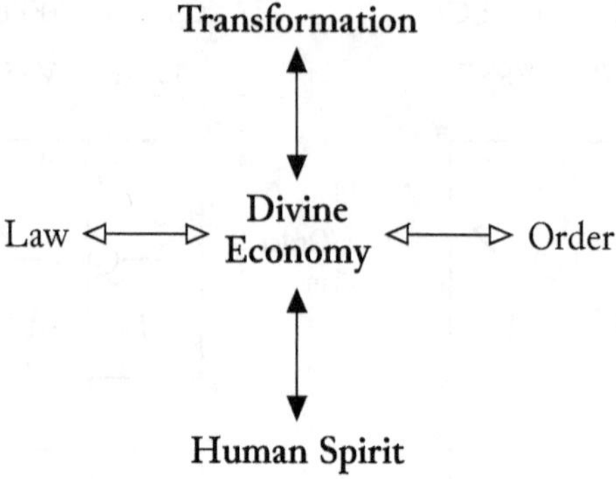

Diagram 3n: The Ethical Strand of the Divine Economy Model

the independent investigation of truth. Equally as significant is the fact that it is because of this entrepreneurship (alertness) that transformation takes place, not only at the level of the individual but also within the economy and within the society. To clarify the importance of justice, it is justice that inextricably links the interests of the individual with those of society. It is, therefore, extremely important for the light of justice to reach and to surround the entire arena of entrepreneurship.

Whoosh! This is now the transition from microeconomics into the realm of ethical economics. The infinite nature of the Nature and Role of Knowledge vector is immutably tied to the Covenant of God. It can be said that God's covenant to humankind is that God would always guide and provide for humankind. That flow (of knowledge and bounty) is essentially infinite (and eternal). Yet it is constrained by the world as we know it. It is this world as we know it and our ability to change it over time that is captured in the Complete Model of the Ethics of the Divine Economy, the third of the series of four models.

To understand the Complete Model of the Ethics of the Divine Economy we first focus our attention on the central, **vertical** axis of the divine economy model (Diagram 3n).

Next, as was developed in detail in ETHICAL ECONOMICS FOR TODAY AND TOMORROW, the model of the ethical economy—confined by its

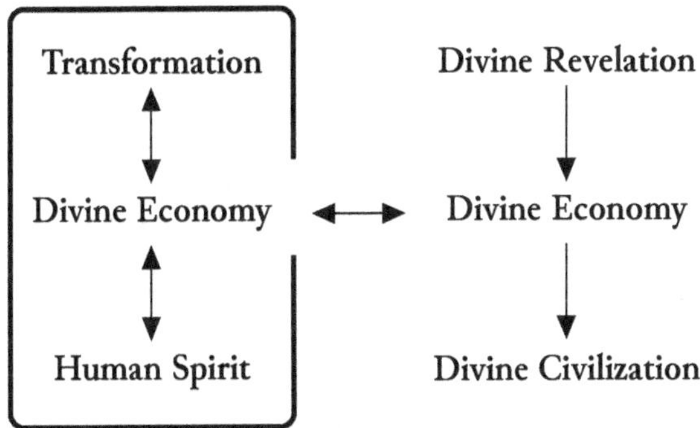

Diagram 3o: Model of the Ethics of the Divine Economy

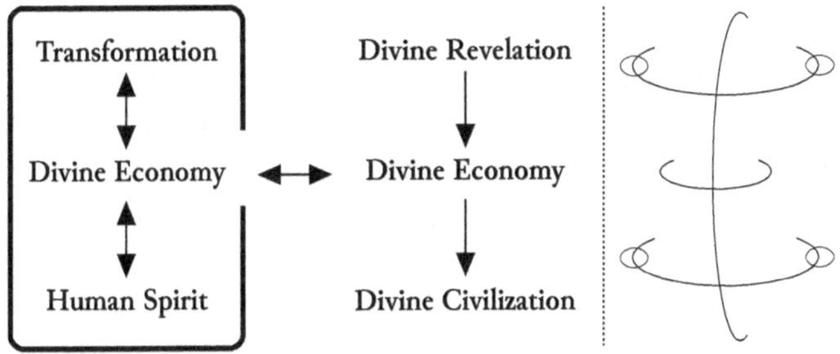

Diagram 3p: Complete Model of the Ethics of the Divine Economy

constraints—is shown as it comes in contact with the ethical knowledge delivered as part of the Covenant of God. Diagram 3o shows how the divine economy is the conduit (divine economy ⟷ divine economy) for the influence of the ethical teachings of the Manifestations of God, to bring about changes at the micro and macro level.

The outcome of divine revelation—which inherently contains knowledge about the divine economy—is a divine civilization.

If not the appearance of a dynamic divine civilization, at least an ever-advancing civilization appears—all depending upon the strength of the Covenant of God in that Day. Diagram 3p shows the Complete Model of the Ethics of the Divine Economy by adding and incorporating the concept of the Covenant of God which is accomplished by incorporating a portion of the symbol of the 'Greatest Name.'

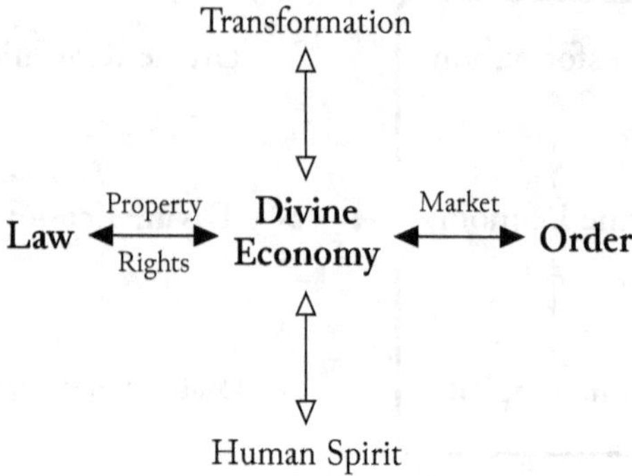

Diagram 3q: The Justice Aspect of the Divine Economy Model

The primary source of ethics required for an ever-advancing civilization comes from the Manifestations of God and it is the impact of Their Teachings that leads to and spiritualizes social cooperation. Again we see the importance of the Covenant when we consider its ability or inability to withstand the assault of the ego-driven. If it is strong and inviolable we get a divine civilization, whereas if it is violated the best we can hope for is an ever-advancing civilization that is constantly being whittled away under the attack of the ego-driven.

Assay

As we move through the sequence of models I think it can be said that we are now feeling a sense of appreciation for and a mounting desire for justice. The divine spark has ignited our alertness to discover and discern justice. It is my job in this chapter and at this point to bring to the forefront the justice aspect of the divine economy model.

If we go back to the skeletal structure of the divine economy model and this time place our focus and emphasis on the central, **horizontal**, Law/Order axis we can begin the process (Diagram 3q).

"The connection between economics and the law is implied, but it is rarely regarded by economists as a special object worthy of their research." Keeping in mind the concept of reciprocity, the immediate implication is that laws bring about order. The source of the laws

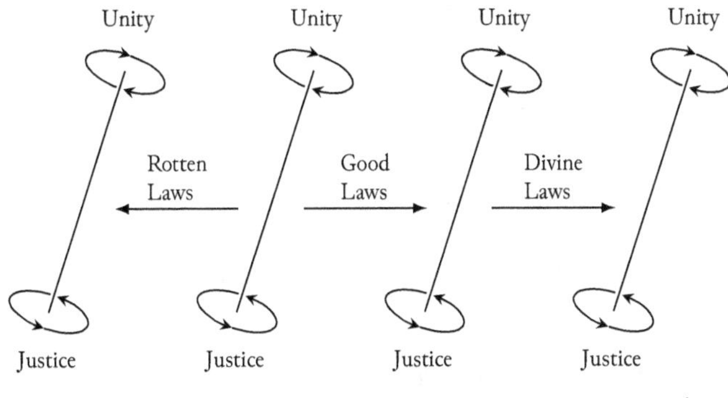

Diagram 3r: Ego-Driven Versus Divine Laws

determines the type of order. Rotten law/order brings about rotten order/law, whereas good law brings about a good order, and whereas divine law brings about divine order (Diagram 3r).

Already clearly identified in the divine economy model is the starting point for laws—property rights. The essence of property rights is this identity: property rights are human rights and human rights are property rights. In other words, the human reality is the most precious of all considerations.

The principal provider of order and of social cooperation—operating and expressed through the language of exchange activities—that fills the lives of everyone everywhere as part of the market process, is the 'market' itself.

Justice implies protective respect for both the human reality and for the healthy freedom of expression of the human reality. To get a better grasp of all of these things—honoring the human reality and its expression—we need to acknowledge the inseparability of liberty and justice. Balancing liberty and justice is the essential key.

And so, necessarily, there is a very meaningful relationship between law and the inseparability of liberty and justice. Developed law, over time, resulting from search and discovery (only if it has been uninfluenced by the ego-driven) is compatible with both liberty and justice.

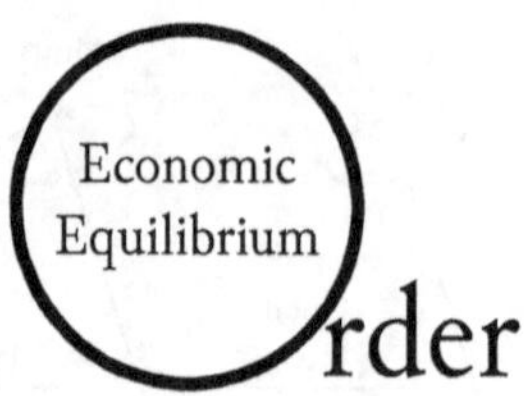

Diagram 3s: The Order of Economic Equilibrium

Probably you or I do not believe that is what we have. But let's assume that is what has occurred and then have fun with that assumption. Liberty and justice create order and having order leads to the refinement of liberty and justice. This cycle is circular just like the letter O in the word 'Order' and according to the divine economy theory the circle is the symbol of economic equilibrium (Diagram 3s).

Although this ideal equilibrium process just described is valid, the starting point is not. In fact, laws have been influenced by the ego-driven and the whole structure of society is the rotten fruit of those laws. The laws need erased, and understandably, the structures built upon those laws are of no value.

Of course replacing the laws and its structures with nothing or just replacing the laws and its structures with a different set of ego-driven laws and structures makes no sense. Only if the Covenant of God provides us with a divine alternative can we be better off than we are now. It is this rational insight that is the foundation of a true human society.

In the Complete Model of the Ethics of the Divine Economy (Diagram 3p) we saw the incorporation of the Covenant of God. At that point only a portion of the 'Greatest Name' was used. What happens if we add the divine microeconomy concept of the divine spark? Remember the radial symmetry of the divine spark? It represents the radial symmetry of the human temple (the head, two arms, and two legs [Diagram 3t]).

Symbolically, it is the divine spark that ignites the human spirit.

Before completing the Model of the Justice of the Divine Economy I want to show you the rest of the 'Greatest Name', and describe how it fits into the model (Diagram 3u).

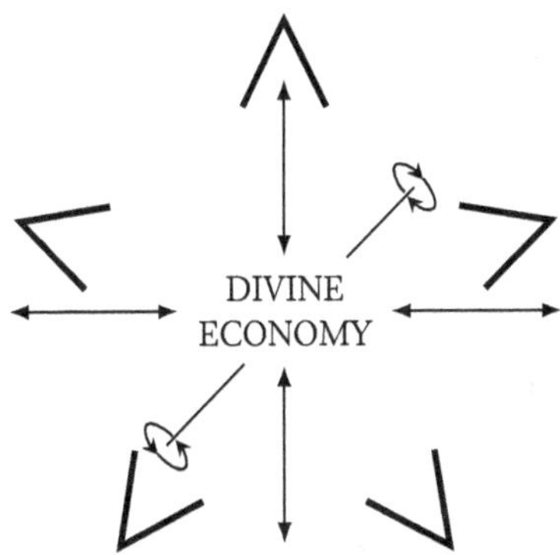

Diagram 3t: The Symmetry of the Divine Spark

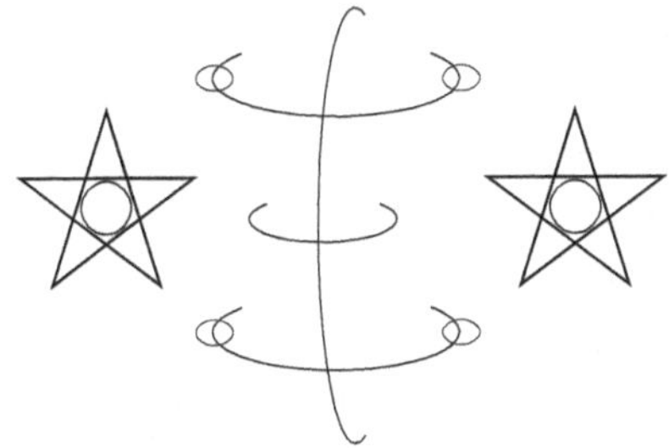

Diagram 3u: The Greatest Name

Notice the two stars. Initially think of them as fulfilling the central, horizontal, Law/Order axis of the divine economy model; the left one representing Law and the right representing Order. But actually these stars historically represent the Twin Manifestations of God in this Day and so they do indeed connect us very specifically to the Covenant of God. Now we can return to continue with the Law/Order analogy. The Laws that They brought will bring the Order of a divine civilization because the Covenant is strong and inviolable, unlike in the past.

With all of this in mind I now present to you the Model of the Justice of the Divine Economy, the fourth of the series of four models.

In contrast to the Complete Model of the Ethics of the Divine Economy (Diagram 3p) notice that Law appears in the leftmost portion of the model and as the leftmost star in the 'Greatest Name' (Covenant)

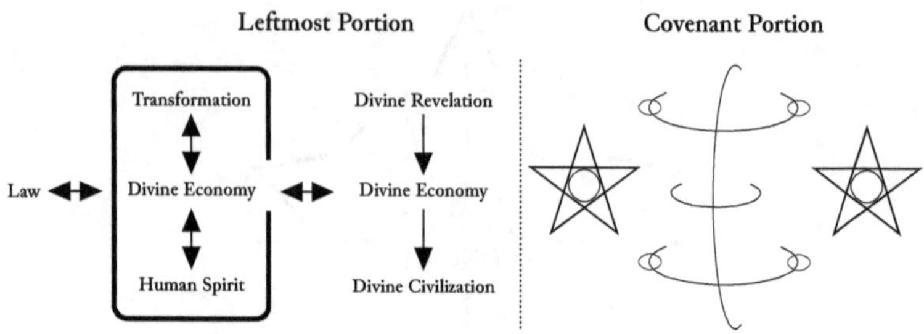

Diagram 3v: The Complete Model of the Justice of the Divine Economy

portion. Also because Law and Order are both a part of the rightmost Covenant portion of the model (the left and right stars, respectively) take notice that the other appearance of Order is in the leftmost portion as part of the divine civilization process (DR→DE↔DC). It turns out that justice is the key ingredient opening a pathway of reciprocity between the divine economy and the divine civilization and vice versa.

The 'Greatest Name' emblem by itself can easily be imagined as a seal to be pressed into wax to seal the deal. This conceptualization fits well with the concept of a covenant (agreement) and it also fits well with the concept of a contractual society. In other words, the economy operates properly when it is contractual.

To close this chapter we bring back the sequence of Diagrams 3a to 3d but complete it using all of the knowledge thus far contained in this chapter.

Diagram 3w shows the progression of thought from the initial concept of the divine economy as a synonym for economic equilibrium to its coming in contact with the human civilization elements of liberty and justice. It becomes clear that liberty and justice are maintained in relative balance by the forces of economic equilibrium, and are contemporarily forced to work against the ego-driven forces. The perfect balance of liberty and justice in the divine economy is the result of the removal of ego-driven intervention, replaced providentially with the divine laws and order provided by the strong and inviolable Covenant given to us in this Day.

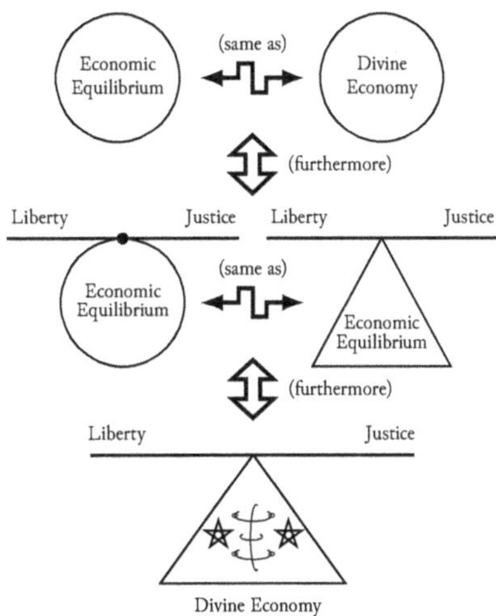

Diagram 3w: The Liberty and Justice of the Divine Economy Sequence

Regarding the divine economy theory I refer you to a quote from Ludwig von Mises, "What matters is not whether a doctrine is new, but whether it is sound." Imagine the benefits to the economy and to human civilization that will result from a healthy injection of both certitude and certainty!

Statement: Now you know the importance of economic freedom.

See What Happens When You Take These Action Steps:

- Be observant of the connection between rotten laws and rotten order.
- Regard contracts as covenants.
- Implant the model visualizations in this book in your mind so you can better apply economics in your life.
- Appreciate the potency of economic equilibrium. Trust in its power to bring about reciprocity, harmony, and balance to the world.

Epilogue

Why is the divine economy model important for you? Because it enhances your vision.

Visualization is a key to the door of understanding and keenness of understanding is due to the keenness of vision. That is what models offer. Of course models have to be representative of reality and these models of the divine economy theory fully appreciate our subjective nature and our spiritual powers. This is certainly an advancement in economic science.

We never stop learning, and these models are not mere objects but rather they are conceptual and dynamic. Every time you revisit these models you will gain something new. That is one of the organic features of these models. Compatibility with your learning process makes these models practical and enriching.

Is it necessary to know the theory that accompanies these models? The answer is yes and no! Just like the benefits you gain from being aware of these models there are benefits from connecting the models with the theory. Economics is not some dry, sterile orthodoxy like it is presented contemporarily. It is vital and magnificent and illuminating which is what the theory around each of these models makes evident. So the answer to the question is not as simple as 'yes or no'. It is about fullness and fulfillment for you. What is your goal?

Along those lines, I encourage you to read the books that contain the models. Each one is about one hundred pages long and is written as a narrative. The theory leads up to the model and then it spreads out into life in the real world. I would love to hear how it changes your perceptions and perspectives. Even though I wrote the theory and discovered the models I learn something new each and every time I revisit the material.

Your friend,

Bruce

All of the books are available on Amazon:

More Than Laissez-Faire
The Human Essence of Economics
Ethical Economics for Today and Tomorrow
Liberty and Justice of Economic Equilibrium

https://www.amazon.com/Bruce-Koerber/e/B00OE2AE7O

Please share your thoughts and comments with me:

Bruce Koerber
divineeconomyconsulting@gmail.com

www.ingramcontent.com/pod-product-compliance
Lightning Source LLC
LaVergne TN
LVHW010841120826
845149LV00020B/3431